The Jack Russell or
Working Terrier

The Jack Russell or Working Terrier

BETTY SMITH

H. F. & G. WITHERBY LTD

First published in Great Britain 1969

This revised edition first published 1990 by
H. F. & G. WITHERBY LTD
14 Henrietta Street, London WC2E 8QJ

© H. F. & G. WITHERBY 1990

Photographs have been kindly supplied by the following:
D. Bottomley, Gordon Craddock, Bert Hardy, John Marchington,
Nicholas Meyjes, Neil Nimmo and ICI, A. F. Stevens,
John Tarlton and Ian Tolputt.

A CIP Catalogue record for this book
is available from the British Library

ISBN 0 85493 199 6

Typeset by CentraCet, Cambridge
and printed in Great Britain by
St Edmundsbury Press Ltd, Bury St Edmunds, Suffolk

Contents

FOREWORD
Wilson Stephens
(formerly Editor, *The Field*)

The best proof of the enduring truths of Mrs Smith's book lies in the fact that after 20 years it remains the acknowledged manual on its subject. Although she is now dead, her insight into the game little dogs of which she wrote, and her sterling good sense about them, live on after her. As the writer of the Foreword to the original and the second editions, it is my privilege to introduce the third. This I do, with warmth and enthusiasm, welcoming it as the message and also the memorial of a great and much loved lady.

Not all of what I wrote in 1970 has stood the test of time as well as her text has done. Though the Jack Russell terrier, and those associated terriers that approximate to it, continue to uphold their ancestors' heritage, the times in which we and they live have changed. This Foreword must take account of the impact of those changes on the terriers themselves, and consequent adjustments to their destiny.

It is still true that where sporting people gather they also take their dogs, and that at point-to-points, gymkhanas, hunter trials, and other occasions at which the country set meet, the working terriers known to many as Jack Russells generally outnumber all the long-recognised breeds added together. They remain a cult among people who know their stuff about the countryside.

The life-style of working earth dogs likewise continues to be what it always was, an underground movement if ever there was one. The digging into the unknown, the confrontation with fox, rat or rabbit, the outfacing and eviction of the enemy (let us not mince words), comprise hard physical work, concentration, determination, stamina, guts and initiative. These qualities are necessarily exercised in solitude and darkness without the aid, support or guidance of a human partner. Often they are called upon in harsh climatic conditions, and after other considerable bodily exertions. Their role has the self-evident social and economic value of pest destruction, the elimination of creatures detrimental to mankind or to farming.

Meeting these demands is obviously easier for a terrier which is well-formed physically for its purposes—not merely a pocket Hercules, but of suitable and balanced conformation. But no degree of physical attributes is the slightest use if the will to employ them is absent. The worth of a Jack Russell is not mainly in the body but very largely in the soul; it is not to be expressed in appearance, but by his character.

This raises what was a burning question in Betty Smith's lifetime, and remains incandescent now, whether or not Kennel Club recognition and suzerainty should be sought for 'the breed'. Here time has moved on. Attempts to obtain recognition have been made and, to the relief of some and the disappointment of others, did not at first make progress. There were solid causes for this, and the Kennel Club could not be blamed.

The Club was confronted by a nationwide population of assorted terriers, many of happy-go-lucky ancestry, to which the names Jack Russell or hunt or working terrier were indiscriminately applied. Hence no identifiable 'breed' existed in the sense of a validated line of terriers which reproduce true to their recorded ancestry, although some private strains may do so. Nor is there still anything more than a sectarian agreement on what a 'Jack Russell' terrier should look like. The latter requirement is mandatory to obtaining Kennel Club recognition, but has been of no consequence to most owners of Jack Russells hitherto, and understandably continues to be opposed by many.

The facts are that appearance has been a matter of individual preference, or of functional suitability for a particular aspect of terrier work (for example, the ideal ratter certainly would not closely resemble the ideal fox-bolter). Those who value their liberty to possess such terriers as they prefer heavily outnumber those who believe that all terriers should be identical.

Consequently the Jack Russell, or the hunt terrier, or the working terrier could not be 'recognised' by the Kennel Club, to whom appearances are paramount and irrespective of actual worth. None of these names implies a breed, a type, or even a community of terriers distinctive enough to be deemed genetically separate from any others. It may be, however, that such a distinctive type is now emerging, thanks to selective breeding, and in 1990 the Kennel Club extended recognition to those on the private register of the Parson Jack Russell Terrier Club, and their progeny. The word 'Parson' in the title solved the problem of nomenclature in establishing separation from the other unrecognised terriers.

What happens hereafter will be eagerly watched by all who read this book in years to come. Misgivings were quickly expressed by the Jack Russell Terrier Club of Great Britain, which had opposed registration, and by the Fox Terrier Club, which has a record of registration as old as the Kennel Club itself. Experience has established that any livestock to which a breed standard is applied thereafter deteriorates. This has been demonstrated by the consequences of applying breed standards to horses, cattle, sheep, pigs, poultry, racing pigeons and cage-birds, with adverse consequences in all cases, as well as to dogs. In their case it has been convincingly demonstrated that only performance tests maintain a viable type, as witness the English springer spaniel in which those bred on the 'handsome is as handsome does' principle retain a physique suitable for their function, whereas those bred to fit the breed standard (or rather the interpretation of it by judges unfamiliar with the spaniel function in practice) become progressively less so. The same could be expected if terriers were required to conform to a physical pattern, and to be judged by people inexperienced in working them.

My expectation is that a small proportion of Jack Russell, working, or hunt terriers, having now been adapted to a breed standard, and given a particular designation, will enable their owners to win prizes at shows. That their descendants will inevitably deteriorate as practical earth dogs will not detract from the pleasure of those who indulge in this meaningless enthusiasm; and good luck to them, they are entitled to their pursuit of happiness as they think fit.

This will not constitute a national disaster, nor harm the general run of earth dogs. The rest of us will continue to possess and enjoy whatever stamp of terriers we best like, and to call them whatever we please. In this we would be faithful to the spirit of natural tolerance in which Betty Smith wrote this excellent, and perhaps immortal, book.

Wilson Stephens
January 1990

Chapter 1

WHY A JACK RUSSELL?

The superior virtues of small, handy, white, or light-coloured, game hunt terriers struck me like a thunderbolt one lovely late November morning in the Border Hills.

I had a broken leg at the time, and was following the Duke

Rough and smooth-coated types of Jack Russell Terrier.

of Buccleuch's foxhounds in a car with George Summers, the huntsman, who, by one of those curious coincidences that occur so frequently amongst people who ride to hounds or ski, also had a broken leg, so we were both unmounted.

Thanks to Summers' genius at knowing just what any fox will do, and to my far-from-skilful driving, we had stolen a march on everyone else, and were now parked on a drove road somewhere between Yetholm and Morebattle, at a point where he assured me the fox would cross about fifty yards ahead.

It was a still frosty day, with intermittent sunshine, and the bracken was golden brown. I had switched off the car engine, and we were just sitting there, listening to the distant bursts of hound music gradually drawing nearer.

In those days I was married to a Border sheep-farmer (I still am married to him, as a matter of fact, but he is no longer a Border sheep-farmer), and we bred Border Terriers for the local hunts. I had two of them in the back of the car, with all the windows open.

Suddenly, George gripped my arm and whispered: 'See him? There he is!'

And there he was—just about the exact spot prophesied—standing in the middle of the roadway, and apparently in no immediate hurry.

Then he bounded on and downhill through the bracken. At that moment, the terriers spotted him, and hurled themselves through the nearest window in pursuit. I managed to grab one, but the other eluded me and was off.

Summers swore and I yelled frantically, but it was too late. Holding tightly onto the remaining terrier, while he hastily wound up the windows, I watched aghast while the fox burst from the bracken and crossed the valley with the small red-brown terrier not twenty yards behind. Just then a burst of music sounded close in our ears, and hounds streamed across the road hot on the scent. It was only then that my heart stopped beating as I realised how terribly like a fox the terrier looked. Would she get chopped by mistake?

If only, I thought desperately, Border Terriers were WHITE—or some obviously un-foxy colour! And how utterly stupid of me to breed anything so likely to be mistaken for a fox. Holding the struggling survivor in my arms, I hoped against hope that the pack would lose the scent in the bracken—but the sterns waved through in a horribly purposeful way, and streamed across the valley. By this time the hunt was crossing the road and plunging down the hill.

Then to my exquisite joy and relief, I saw them going up the hill on the far side, with the fox still well ahead, hounds next and a small red labouring body panting well in the rear, but still keeping her end up.

'Wake up, lassie,' said Summers, 'and get a move on. He'll be making for the Curr. We want to get down on to the lower road now. I'll tell you where to turn.'

'I must get hold of that terrier,' I said.

'Och—she'll come home herself—never heed her. Now if you turn left here, there should be a cart track that'll take us down through Cherrytrees. Step on it!'

Well, Vicky turned up all right, none the worse for her hunt, but from that day on I was obsessed with the idea of breeding small white terriers that could not possibly be mistaken for foxes in any circumstances. I think it was my father-in-law who first recommended Jack Russells, as a breed he had known and admired for years. He had a large and comprehensive sporting library, and together we searched the shelves for books that would enable me to glean any available information. I returned home with the back of the car stacked with miscellaneous volumes, and my ears full of strict orders to return them all in good order and as soon as possible.

My literary research was surprisingly disappointing. There were lots of anecdotes about Parson Jack Russell himself, and quite a comprehensive life history of that remarkable man, but the Jack Russell Terrier itself seemed to peter out after his death.

Still, I argued, there must be some terriers still extant descended from the original stock, if I could only find out where, and how to get hold of them.

Normally, with a registered breed, I would write to the Kennel Club and ask for the name and address of the Breed Club Secretary, who would then send me the names and addresses of the nearest reliable breeders on the Club list, but here again I found myself against a snag. Jack Russells are not a registered breed with the Kennel Club. So I had to depend upon the local grapevine.

Now the grapevine is a curious thing, and news travels along with remarkable celerity through devious routes that leave Alph, the sacred river, looking like the Manchester Ship Canal on a wet Monday. Not only news—bowler hats as well. I once had an unmarked bowler—anonymous, size six and three-quarters, steel-lined, made by Cunningham—blown off my head in a truly howling gale on the top of an unidentified (by me, anyway) Cheviot about twenty miles from home and over the English border, while hunting with the College Valley Hounds. As I was riding at full gallop at the time, with hounds running hard, I did not stop to pick it up, and the last I saw of it, out of the corner of my eye, it was bowling away merrily on its brim downhill towards Wooler. Next morning, I wired to Cunningham for a new one—but to my incredulous amazement, my bowler, beautifully brushed and clean, was handed in that very evening by one of the shepherds. I never really got the whole story, but they said that it had been picked up by the shepherd of the out-bye hirsel we had been galloping over, after the hunt had passed. The shepherd next door told him that there had been a lassie without a hat riding with the hunt when it passed him. Yet another shepherd said that would likely be yon

A Jack Russell Terrier bitch (*left*) and dog (*right*). Note the heavier look of the dog and, in both, the typical digging paws.

young Mistress Smith frae Clifton Cote, and my hat had passed from hand to hand and hirsel to hirsel until it finally reached home in remarkably swift time.

Once word went round that Betty Smith had suddenly gone mad and wanted a Jack Russell, news of litters from miles around began to filter in. My neighbours lifted their eyebrows and shrugged their shoulders, and prophesied that this latest craze would not last long. Border Terriers were the breed. All the local and neighbouring hunts had always used them. What was wrong with them? Grand, sturdy, game, tireless little dogs. Nothing wrong with their colour either. It was my head that was wrong. And let them tell *me* that what was good enough for their fathers and grandfathers and great-grandfathers was good enough for them and ought to be good enough for me. Who the hell did I think I was, anyway? Marrying into the Borders like that—and jolly lucky to do so—I should be humbly grateful for what the Borders could provide in such excellent abundance. Jack Russells indeed! A bastard English breed from Devonshire. However, if I persisted in my errant ways, they'd heard that there was a likely litter over by Yarrow way that I could probably get a puppy from for a fiver. But—mind me—it wouldn't be any good.

About the virtues of Border terriers, Border horses, Border men, Border sheep and Border foxhounds, I most humbly and fervently agreed. But I still wanted my Jack Russell Terrier.

So, wilfully abandoning my housework and young, I set off as soon as I could get the car, to inspect the nearest litters. These proved extremely elusive, as nobody seemed to have an address, far less a telephone number. The grapevine would assure me that there was a litter belonging to a chap up by Yarrow. I couldn't miss the place (couldn't I just?), as it was just up beyond the kirk, no mare'n a mile or twa. The Scottish mile is a peculiarly elastic measure, as I found to my cost. It just goes on and on and on, and every time one stops and asks, one's objective seems just as far ahead as it was the last time. One's only consolation is that at least the ruddy place isn't actually gaining on one.

However, I did run one or two litters of alleged Jack Russells to the ground, but they were a sad disappointment. 'Jack Russell', in the south of Scotland, seemed to be a generic term covering a multitude of canine sins, ranging from slip-ups between a collie and a Sealyham to mistakes between a Dandy Dinmont and a foxhound. They came in all shapes, sizes and colours.

I patiently explained to every hopeful owner that what I wanted was a small terrier, white in colour, or white with black or tan markings, but predominantly white, not too short in the leg, rough or smooth, but preferably rough, and weighing about twelve pounds. If I had said that I wanted a unicorn with pink spots they could not have been more surprised. *That* wasn't a Jack Russell. *These* were Jack Russells, and I wouldn't find any better.

By this time my blood was up and I was determined to find the Jack Russell of my dreams—even if I had to traipse all over Devon.

Then, to my great joy, I was asked to judge at a dog-show in Dumfriesshire, run by the local agricultural society by sanction of the Kennel Club. Sanction shows are different from the normal Kennel Club sponsored shows (Championship, Open, or Members) as they may legitimately include unregistered dogs, and I was thrilled to find that there were classes for Shepherd's Collies, Gamekeeper's dogs *and Jack Russell Terriers* on the agenda. However, once more, they came in all shapes, colours and sizes—the most popular being what looked to me like a cross between a Border Terrier and a Lakeland. They were black and tan in colour, and obviously keen and game and round, but—not my idea of a Jack Russell.

It was after the judging was over, and I was being entertained at the bar, that I learnt that no true Jack Russell has a pedigree. Having been brought up with pedigreed, Kennel-Club-registered dogs all round me from birth, I was deeply and profoundly shocked at this heresy. It wasn't only dogs—I was accustomed to horses in the Stud Book, cattle in the Herd Book, and sheep in the Flock Book. Even my Persian kitten had a pedigree, and, for all I knew, was entered in some Feline Bible somewhere.

'But how can you possibly tell if it is a pure-bred Jack Russell if it hasn't a pedigree, and if its parents and ancestors are not registered?' I asked, aghast.

This led to some uncomplimentary remarks about the

Kennel Club, and what happened to every single breed they got their hands on. I was implored to look at what they'd done to the Fox Terrier, to the Lakeland, to the Welsh, to the Airedale, to the Sealyham, to the— Here I interrupted smartly to point out that the Border, although registered and fully pedigree for generations, and widely shown at Kennel Club shows all over the place, was still the old original type.

They graciously granted me the Border Terrier, but refused me all other terriers, until I was reduced to feeble ejaculations of 'Yes—but—' whenever I could get a word in edgewise.

However, they left me with the clear impression that only over their communal dead bodies would the Jack Russell ever be a registered Kennel Club breed. I still think it a pity, as registration has its points, which I hope to deal with in a later chapter. Meanwhile, it still occupies the unique position—years later than this occasion—of being one of the most popular and widely-sought-after breeds that yet remains outside the Kennel Club pale.

Chapter 2

PRESSING ON REGARDLESS

It was not until we moved from our hill sheep farm in the Borders to the richer, kinder, arable land of the Lothians that I found Jack Russell Terriers, as I knew them, in any amount. And even then they were kept mostly as pets, or for ratting, and were mostly English imports. The Lothians are not, on the whole, hunting counties, but there is one pack that hunts mostly in West Lothian—the Linlithgow and Stirlingshire— and here the Jack Russell does come into his own as a hunt terrier.

By this time, I was not only really keen on the breed, which has a character all of its own, combining gaiety, intelligence, lovingness, faithfulness, a keen sense of humour, and a wonderfully reliable temperament, with toughness, grit, gameness, quickness, a tremendous capacity for unflagging keenness and hard work, as well as good nose and eye—but I was becoming more and more impressed by their all-round suitability for almost any home or job. I think that this is the real secret of their ever-increasing popularity. They are a canine multum in parvo—small dogs with big hearts, and tremendously adaptable.

They are neat, clean, and easily house-trained, yet they will live quite happily in outside kennels. They are sporting, and naturally prefer country life, or life on a farm, but they can be kept happily and healthily in a town flat. They can

Four rough-coated Jack Russells used by the Tyndale Hunt
in the 1960s.

even be trained not to chase cats, or rather to live in perfect
harmony with the household cats, and will curl up with them
on the rug, or armchair or sofa or in front of the kitchen fire,
depending upon their owners' ideas about a dog's place.
They are no more aggressive towards other dogs than any
terrier, and quickly learn not to fight, if one starts young
enough. On the other hand they are utterly fearless and will
tackle anything, at the drop of a hat, from a St Bernard to a
badger, and give a very good account of themselves in the
process.

Being small and nippy, they can dodge like lightning, and
have a grip like a bear-trap. They are wonderful guards, and
will willingly defend their owners or their owners' belongings
to the death. Yet they are wonderful with children—
especially babies, and I have never yet known a Jack Russell

bite a child—even if the child richly deserved to be bitten. I have several times 'rescued' a Jack Russell from the clutches of an importunate two-year-old, whose idea of loving was to seize the dog in a merciless grip—often upside down—and squeeze the breath out of it, only to have it come back for more, and apparently enjoy it.

Much as I hate to see a Jack Russell turned by doting old dames into a lap-dog, I must confess that it seems to enjoy that too, although to see it at its best you want to watch it go to ground after a fox, or explore a ditch or a conduit on a country walk, or enjoying the ecstatic raptures of catching rats at the bottom of a stack at an old-fashioned threshing.

To watch a couple of good Jack Russells hunting a hedgerow or a bank or a ditch is sheer joy, as they seem to be so completely and intuitively *en rapport*. Bright-eyed, ears cocked, with their little wet legs looking like matchsticks, filthy dirty, and with their coats sticky with burrs, they work together as if controlled by one mind. Little escapes them. Tongues out, panting with excitement, and occasionally uttering short sharp yelps of joy, they are absolutely tireless. They can come home after a really hard day, settle down for a short nap after their evening feed, and be all agog for another walk or hunt in the evening. They will also exercise themselves for hours on end by playing together, or hunting imaginary rats in a rat-free garden. In fact, this capacity for make-believe, if they cannot get at the real thing, is one of their most endearing characteristics. Two Jack Russells are always, of course, better than one Jack Russell, but even one Jack Russell will never be bored. He will amuse himself for hours with an old stocking—and will obviously pretend it is a rat—toss it up in the air, catch it, worry it, chase it, push it around with his nose, paw at it, and finally tear it to bits and come and ask wistfully for another.

Personally, I dislike teaching dogs tricks, and I strongly disapprove of titbits at mealtimes, but I must admit that the

Jack Russell can beg in the most endearing, coaxing and pathetic manner that can melt the most adamant heart. I also know of one, at least, who belongs to a family of children, with a repertoire of tricks that would earn their fortune in a circus or on the halls.

I also know one that fetches the morning post for his owners, but who considers the morning paper his own special prerogative, in spite of all efforts on their part to convince him that he is mistaken. He invariably succeeds in snatching it away and flying off, pursued by frantic yells and vituperation, until, grinning all over his face, he finally yields it—but only when he is tired of the game.

Jack Russells have the most amazingly expressive ears, which they can move up and down like no other dog, and with which they can almost talk. They have been aptly described by one owner as 'butterfly ears', which is a good description, as they do 'butterfly'.

They are also wonderful car dogs, and adore motoring. They like to see where they are going, and take an incessant interest, which one of our terriers kept up for over two hundred miles on one occasion without flagging. To quote from a letter, 'so many of them like to sit in the little space behind the back window, or else on your lap while you drive. Mine sits bolt upright, looking through the steering-wheel and out through the window. She is a complete contrast to my old and servile spaniel who will travel anything up to one hundred miles lying down. One of the joys and, of course, disadvantages, is the curiosity and interest in life that these little beasts have.'

They are also wonderful guards, and if you own a Jack Russell you never need to lock your car, as nobody is allowed in until you return.

Jack Russell barks intrigue me, as they have a tremendous gamut of expression. In fact, once you learn their language, they can talk.

On a country walk they will run ahead, hunting the hedgerows and ditches, uttering occasional short, shrill yelps of sheer excitement. When they come to a likely hole or a conduit, they will sniff, then bark to let their companions know there is something at home, then go round quickly to the other side to start a pincer movement, all the time whimpering: 'Hurry! Hurry!'

If they need human assistance, the barking becomes loud and persistent, with a curiously urgent note, with short pauses between the barks. If, on the other hand, they find something wrong and requiring immediate attention—such as an 'owled' sheep, or a cow or pony in trouble in a bog the barking assumes a totally different note, not so shrill, and less of a yap, but persistent and penetrating. A terrier that has got stuck underground has a different bark again—and enough sense to keep on barking until it knows that help is at hand. And I swear that it is possible to tell, from the bark alone, whether the terrier is in an empty hole, or whether it has got stuck with a fox or a badger.

In the house, it is possible to tell whether a Jack Russell has got shut inside a room and wants out, or is shut outside wanting in. Either way, he'll let you know.

A Jack Russell has also a most charming repertoire of noises to gain admittance. You are probably comfortably ensconced in an armchair by the fire, or watching television, and in no mind to get up and let him in. He knows this. So first there is a gentle scratch, very soft and sweet, just to let you know he is there. Then, after a pause, there is another scratch, and a little pathetic whimper. Then another pause, while he waits with his ears cocked, probably one paw raised, listening to see if that has moved you. If it hasn't, he will bark, once or twice, tentatively, just to remind you that it is cold outside in the passage and he is getting impatient. If you still remain adamant, he will attack the door violently, scrabbling at the paintwork with both fore-feet, barking at intervals meanwhile. And that *does* fetch you. Probably furious, but it is your own fault for not getting up sooner. When you open the door, frequently with some violence, and possibly cursing him for being a nuisance and ruining the paint, he shoots in, turns round two or three times, and then leaps into your arms. You can't be cross after that.

Of course, Jack Russells differ. I know one that impatiently launches himself at every door he wants to pass through, without any preliminaries, and another that just sits there and barks in a piercing tenor, all on the same note. But the majority work up to their grand climax gradually. Bitches are better at these tactics than dogs. And much more cunning.

It was only when we emigrated from the far cold north to the deep warm south that I found myself right in the heart of the Jack Russell country, where almost everyone kept one or bred them. Although they vary slightly in size and coat and length of leg, some being smooth and some rough and some in between the two, while some have markings and some haven't, they are all instantly recognisable as gen-U-ine Jack Russells, and they all share the same superb qualities.

Around here, too, pedigrees are kept, and certain blood-lines are sought above others, as the progenitors have all had a reputation for being everything a Jack Russell should be.

Puppies generally run very true to type, and litters are beautifully level, with little to choose between one puppy and another.

A rather curious phenomenon, however, is that if by mischance a bitch contracts a mésalliance, her progeny generally take strongly after mum. This was especially evident in the case of a great friend of mine called Tumpy, who was found to be in whelp—nobody quite knew how, but there she was—swelling visibly, like a little sausage balloon, and obviously very pleased with herself. As there were no male Jack Russells in the immediate neighbourhood, her owners were naturally worried. Potential sires were (a) one

Rabbiting in the New Forest.

of my Bull-mastiffs (but unlikely), (b) Mr Dykes's Welsh Collie (*very* likely), (c) the stationmaster's black Labrador (possible), (d) Mr Morgan's collie (possible), (e) Mrs Cooper's Fox Terrier (we hoped), (f) an indeterminate and underfed-looking white terrier of doubtful breeding and appalling habits, given to bolting like a hare if anyone spoke to him, however kindly, who was reputed to come from somewhere up the back lane.

As D-day approached (date necessarily a trifle uncertain), we all waited anxiously to see what Tumpy would bring forth. She kept her secret well, as when the puppies eventually arrived, with consummate ease and a few days earlier than expected, they all looked exactly like Tumpy.

Chapter 3

TYPE AND TEMPERAMENT

The prototype and progenitress of the Jack Russell Terriers was a little bitch called Trump, bought from a milkman that their founder met on the Marston road while still an undergraduate at Oxford.

There is a glorious description of this historic occasion in an old book published in 1883 by Richard Bentley & Sons –

The REV.D JACK RUSSELLS First Terrier.

This portrait of Parson Jack Russell's terrier Trump hangs in the harness room at Sandringham.

Memoirs of the Rev. John Russell of Tordown, by one Mr Davis—which is well worth quoting in full:

> It was a glorious afternoon towards the end of May when strolling round Magdalen Meadow with Horace in hand, but Beckford in his head, he emerged from the classic shade of Addison's Walk, crossed the Cherwell in a punt, and passed over in the direction of Marston, hoping to devote an hour or two to study in the quiet meads of that hamlet, near the charming slopes of Elsfield, or in the deeper and more secluded haunts of Shotover Wood. But before he reached Marston a milkman met him with a terrier—such an animal as Russell had only yet seen in his dreams; he halted, as Actaeon might have done when he caught sight of Diana disporting in her bath; but unlike that ill-fated hunter, he never budged from the spot till he had won the prize and secured it for his own. She was called Trump, and became the progenitress of that famous race of terriers which, from that day to the present, have been associated with Russell's name at home and abroad— his able and keen coadjutors in the hunting field.

Russell's own description of Trump might well stand for a blue-print of the breed: 'Her colour was white, with just a patch of dark tan over each ear and a similar dot not larger than a penny piece over the root of her tail. The coat, which was thick, close and a trifle wavy, was well calculated to protect the body from the wet and cold. The legs were straight, short and thick, and the feet perfect, while the size was equal to that of a full-grown vixen fox, that is to say, her weight was about twelve pounds. Her whole appearance gave indications of courage, endurance, and hardihood.'
Davis enlarges on this description by saying that the coat was 'thick, close and a trifle wiry . . . but has no affinity with

the long, rough jacket of a Scotch Terrier: the loins and whole frame indicative of hardihood and endurance.'

There are, to-day, two schools of thought as regards coats. Some people prefer the smooth, as being cleaner, more easily kept free of burrs and tangles, quicker to dry, and also making it easier to find and dress cuts and wounds. They say that the smooth-coats are no less hardy than the roughs, and do not seem to feel the cold and wet any more. Both types are tacitly recognised as Jack Russell.

The reference to short legs may be misleading to those who think of Sealyhams or Dachshunds. In her portrait Trump is not particularly short in the leg, but proportioned rather like a Border Terrier—rather longer than she is tall.

The fox, both in size and proportion, is a fairly accurate model—and where a fox can go, a terrier can follow. Short legs are actually a disadvantage if a terrier has to run with hounds or cover long distances with a horse.

Neither a terrier nor a fox walks into an earth—they crouch down and creep in, or dig their way in. And, as Mr Dan Russell once remarked: 'Have you ever seen a short-legged fox?'

Temperament, however, is far more important than looks. A Jack Russell may be the Adonis of his breed, but if he hasn't the temperament—the heart and guts—the hardihood and the courage—he is about as useless as a Rolls-Royce without oil and petrol. He also needs to combine courage with discretion, as a dog whose courage is of the foolhardy, reckless type, and who rushes in bald-headed at a fox, is going to be more of a nuisance than he is worth, besides spending half his time out of action owing to wounds and stitches. You will also have to nurse him back to health after almost every tussle. Nor is the dog who rushes in and grips his fox much good. For one thing, he cannot grip and bark, so that you have no idea, up above, where he is or what is going on. His job is to indicate always where he is, and what is going on, and to bolt his fox, or keep it at bay until it can be dug out.

Giving tongue is another great virtue in a Jack Russell, especially in an earth that has many galleries and openings.

Even in rocky country, like the Lake District, where digging is impossible, it is still a good thing to know what your terrier is up to, and where he is—while in soft ground there is nothing more exasperating than to howk energetically for an hour or more to reach a silent terrier, only to find it emerging cheerfully, and as pleased as punch with itself, from another exit!

Courage, of course, is essential, and a cowardly or nervous terrier is of no practical use as a worker.

The over-aggressive terrier is just as big a risk as the obviously nervous or timid one, and I am sure that the root cause is the same—*fear*. The only difference lies in manifestation, as the aggressive dog reckons that attack is the best means of defence. A really courageous dog is seldom aggressive, unless provoked.

Malnutrition or bad rearing, however, can cause some temporary symptoms of timidity in a young puppy that will disappear completely in a matter of weeks, with proper feeding and good handling, so that it is not always easy to tell, when the puppies are still with their dam, whether a timid puppy is a case of under-feeding, nerve-starvation, and rickets, or a dead loss. The bitch is usually a reliable guide, and, of course, so is the sire, if available for inspection. So is the pedigree—if any.

But, on the whole, it is better not to buy a puppy from a litter that you suspect has been undernourished, or reared in a cold, damp, draughty kennel, as even if his temperament turns out to be all right, his physical development has had a shockingly bad start from which it may never fully recover. Those first few weeks are tremendously important.

Intelligence is another vital factor in a good terrier, but I shall deal with this in the next chapter.

Chapter 4

INTELLIGENCE

Courage, soundness, hardihood and good temperament are all directed and improved by intelligence, and in my own dogs I try to breed for this quality above all the rest.

A stupid dog is a boring dog, although he can be amusing at times, but one's amusement is tempered with pity, as the clot is always rather pathetic.

A really intelligent terrier, on the other hand, is a continual joy and a sheer pleasure to work with.

In my opinion, intelligence must be inbred but it can be stunted or developed to a surprising degree by training, by talking to the dog, and by treating it as a companion. Dogs are not merely animals, living by instinct and experience. They are highly developed creatures, who, from thousands of years of close association with man, have become sort of missing links.

Parson Jack Russell understood this very well, and always looked upon his terriers as friends, and treated them as such.

His biographer, Davis, reports that 'Russell looked upon his terriers as his fireside friends—the Penates of his home; nor was he ever happier than when to some congenial spirit he was recording the service they had done him in bygone days; and vast indeed was the store from which he drew so many interesting facts connected with their history.'

One of his dogs, Tip, a descendant of his famous Trump,

was especially remarkable, as he displayed reasoning power far beyond the average. To quote Mr Davis again:

A hundred anecdotes might be related of the wondrous sagacity displayed in the chase by Russell's terriers, but as Tip's name has been already mentioned, one of his many feats will suffice to show, not merely the large amount of instinctive faculty, but the almost reasoning power with which that dog was endowed. [He then goes on to tell the incident in Parson Jack's own words.] On one occasion I found a fox which, in spite of a trimming scent, contrived to beat us by reaching Grey's Holts and going to ground before we could catch him. Now these earths are as fathomless and interminable as the catacombs of St Calixtus. They are so called 'grey' from the old Devonshire name signifying a badger, a number of these animals having long occupied that spot. Consequently such a fortress, once gained, is not easily to be stormed, even by Tip or the stoutest foe.

'Again we found that fox a second time and now, while the hounds were in close pursuit and driving hard, I saw Tip going off at full speed in quite a different direction.

'He's off, sir, to Grey's Holts. I know he is!' shouted Jack Yelland, the whip, as he called my attention to the line of country the dog was then taking.

That proved to be the case. The fox had scarcely been ten minutes on foot when the dog, either by instinct, or as I believe, some power akin to reason, putting two and two together, came to the conclusion that the real object of the fox was to gain Grey's Holts, although the hounds were by no means pointing in that direction. It was exactly as if the dog had said to himself: 'No, no! You're the same fox that gave us the slip once before, but you are not going to play us that trick again.'

Tip's deduction was accurately correct for the fox, after

A rough-coated bitch ready to go into the showring. As Jack Russell Terriers are not recognised as a distinct breed, judges look for good action and signs of the right temperament.

Two more showring hopefuls.

a turn or two in cover, put his nose directly for Grey's Holts, hoping, beyond a doubt, to gain that city of refuge once more, and then to whisk his brush in the face of his foes. But in this manoeuvre he was fairly outgeneralled by the dog's tactics. Tip had taken the short cut—the chord of an arc— and, as hounds raced by at some distance off, there I saw him, dancing about on Grey's Holts, throwing his tongue frantically, and doing his utmost, by noise and gesture, to scare the fox away from approaching the earths. Perfect success crowned the manoeuvre. The fox, not daring to face the lion in his path, gave the spot a wide berth, while the hounds, carrying a fine head, passed on to the heather, and after a clinking run killed him on the open moor.

Tip hardly ever missed a day for several seasons, and, even in his old age, no man on earth could catch him once he had seen Russell with his top boots on.

Then there was the one-eyed Nelson. Russell had run a fox to ground near Tetcott, but tiers of passages, one below the other, made the earth such a honeycomb that the diggers were bewildered, and the terriers puzzled, as there was scent everywhere.

Nelson at length emerged, and, some distance off, began digging eagerly at the grass.

'Here's the fox,' said Russell, 'under Nelson's nose, or I'll forfeit my head.'

Once he saw the men digging over the spot, Nelson left them, and re-entered the earth, 'marking hard and sharp under the very spot'. The diggers dug like furies, and—there was the fox.

I am glad to relate that Parson Jack always gave his dug foxes a very sporting chance, and good start before allowing his well-controlled hounds to follow in pursuit. Although I am by no means anti-blood-sports, it sickens me to see a hunted fox, who has already reached sanctuary, and so, to my way of thinking, has earned the right to rest in peace until another day, dug mercilessly out and flung to the waiting pack, or only given a few feeble yards' start. That, I think, is really cruel and beastly.

Parson Jack Russell's terriers, however, were trained for one object only—hunting the fox, and were 'as steady from riot as the staunchest of his hounds so that, running with them, and never passing an earth without drawing it, they gave the fox, whether above ground or below it, but a poor chance of not being found, either by one or the other. A squeak from a terrier was the sure signal of a find, and there was not a hound in the pack that would not fly to it, as eagerly as to Russell's horn, or to his own wild and marvellous scream.'

Nevertheless, it is interesting to note that the terriers were house-dogs, and 'fireside friends'—and Parson Jack obviously did not share the view, held by so many to-day, that keeping terriers in the house ruins them for work. In my opinion it actually improves them, as their intelligence develops more by being kept as companions and allowed to share the family activities, than it does if they are left to their own resources for long hours in a kennel. They also enjoy sharing the family car—and I have never noticed any lack of keenness or incipient softness as a result. They love being talked to— and although they may not always understand every word, they can certainly understand the gist of what is being said.

They also know when they must stay in the car, such as on Sunday mornings, when the family goes to church, and never attempt to jump out when the door is opened; and when they can join the family, such as on visits to the beach or to certain friends and relations who welcome dogs.

Although it is a common fallacy that brains and beauty are poles apart, I have never found this in the various breeds I have kept, bred and shown, and some of my best working dogs have been show champions.

Chapter 5

STARTING FROM SCRATCH

Possibly because I write for a dog paper, I get a lot of letters from people who want advice about the best way to make a start in the breed of their choice. Sometimes they want to begin breeding seriously, and to start a kennel, but more often they just want to know how to acquire a good dog that they can show, work or breed from—or all three.

In some cases the answer is fairly simple. Go to a reliable kennel, put yourself in the owner's hands, and say that you want a good bitch, suitable for showing and breeding. You will probably have to pay a stiff price for her, but you should get that back from the sale of the first litter. Ask her breeder to recommend a suitable stud dog, and ask someone who knows about the breed to help you to pick the puppy, or puppies, you want to keep.

In the case of aspiring Jack Russell owners, it is not so simple. For one thing, a good Jack Russell bitch is worth her weight in uranium, and if the owners are willing to part with her, they are either nuts, or there is something wrong with the bitch. A good brood bitch is all important—especially as regards temperament and working qualities. Also working bitches are funny—and if they have become really attached to their owners they may not settle well with anyone else. In fact, the better the bitch the more devoted she is, and the more accustomed to working exclusively for one person.

Alert and expectantly awaiting the day's events.

So probably your best bet is a bitch puppy, that you can train to your ways from the very start. By the time she is old enough to breed from, you will have found out all about her, too.

Again, I think the best way is to go to the nearest reliable kennel and explain what you want. If you are an utter novice, don't be ashamed to admit it, or afraid that the breeder will take advantage of your ignorance. Reliable kennels have built up their reputation by satisfied customers, and good dogs, and they know very well that one dissatisfied customer and one bad dog can do them more harm than ten of the other kind can do good.

The dam and her puppies should look clean, well-cared-for, keen, and healthy, and should come to meet their owner with joy, although the bitch may be a bit suspicious of strangers at first.

Prices vary, but at the time of publication you should be

able to buy a good'un from about £45. Unless you spot one that you particularly fancy, it might be as well to let the breeder pick your puppy for you.

If you don't know of any reliable kennels near enough to visit, and are unwilling to buy a puppy unseen, and know of no experienced person who can advise you, probably your best plan is to ask at your local hunt kennels. Failing this, be very careful. See both the sire and the dam, if possible, and ask about their working abilities. A few drinks at the local will often help here, if you go about it tactfully—as a good terrier has generally got a good local reputation.

When I was looking for my first Jack Russell, I went to see all sorts of litters for miles around who were not Jack Russells at all, but just by-blows. In some cases, the dam was not even on view—just the litter—but, of course, I was right out of Russell country.

Don't be in any hurry to pick your puppy, but watch them all playing for a while, and notice which ones are the most alert and keen. Wave your handkerchief at one or two, and see whether they are frightened and back away, or whether they come forward eagerly and try to worry it. Clap your hands suddenly, not too loudly—there's a limit—and see how they react to that. Drop a pencil or a box of matches on the ground and see how their ears go—forward or back.

Don't be shy to ask questions about the sire and dam, such as how keen they are, how often they have been to ground, whether they give good tongue when working, do they run riot, are they sound and healthy? Also is the breeder prepared to give you a written guarantee that his information is correct? Examine the puppy of your final choice before deciding. Be wary of a puppy that piddles as you lift it, as that is a sign of nervousness. Ask if they have been wormed, and how often (it should be twice, for safety); if over three months, whether it has been inoculated against distemper, hardpad and leptospirosis. There should be no discharge from the nose or eyes, nor should its belly be swollen, nor should there be any signs of umbilical hernia (i.e. a swelling around the navel). Look at its mouth—which should be neither overshot nor undershot, but level, with good clean white sharp little teeth, and pink healthy gums. Examine its skin for lice or sores or eczema. The eyes should be dark and bright, and the expression keen. The nose should be black and damp and cool to the touch. Smell the breath too, as this should be fresh and sweet.

Finally, before you depart with it, ask for feeding instructions, as it is easier to keep to the same diet for a time after you get it, and until it settles down in its new surroundings.

If you do not feel competent to do all this yourself, ask if you may have him for at least a fortnight on approval and get a vet to look at him.

If you see a likely older dog advertised it is best to contact the owner first, before going to see the dog or having it sent to you (at your expense), asking the size, weight, age and markings, whether it is dead game, how many times has it been to ground? Does it throw its tongue well? Is it clean, sound, and healthy? Has it been inoculated? And is the owner prepared to guarantee all this? What is the price? Always ask for a month's approval. Most owners are willing for this, and a fortnight does not really give you long enough.

A good made dog of good temperament is generally rather a quiet dog, who will often carry his tail drooping when not in action. He should have a bright dark eye, and be up on his toes. He should not be aggressive or yappy. Give him a day or two to settle down before trying him.

Talk to him quietly and gently, and don't fuss him. Lead him to the earth, show him the hole, but without any excitement or siccing on, slip off his collar and let him go. If he is the right sort he won't need any urging.

Chapter 6

HOUSE-TRAINING

A young puppy has no more control over its bowels and bladder than a young baby has, so that it is extremely stupid and silly of its owner to expect it to be clean until it has cut its second teeth. Reliably clean, that is, although it is possible to avoid any accidents, and train the puppy gradually in good habits, by knowing what to expect, when to expect it, and taking steps accordingly.

The psychological moments are (a) just after waking, (b) after a meal, (c) after a romp or exercise, and (d) after it has been excited.

During the summer months, which are by far the best time to bring up a puppy in the way you hope he will continue, it is a fairly easy matter to catch him before anything awful happens to your best carpet, and pop him out of doors. Stay with him and encourage him until he has performed, and then praise him and bring him indoors again. I always use the same words: 'Hurry up!' (uttered more urgently if it happens to be raining) and 'Clever boy!' or 'Clever girl!' after he or she obliges.

If, however, it is winter time and he wants out in the middle of the night when you are clad only in a nylon nightie, then it is possible to train him to use a pile of newspapers in a corner (always the same corner), or a piece of turf in a box, or a box of earth or cinders.

Needless to say, if you don't want your house to pong to high heaven, these must be kept clean, and changed regularly.

There are certain proprietary 'puppy trainers'—a few drops of which, sprinkled on his loo, are recommended as helping him to understand their function, but I have never used these, or indeed found them necessary. The great thing, even if the puppy ignores his loo at first, is to catch him in the act and pop him on the right spot. Do *not* however, grab him too roughly or quickly, or shout at him, or he will become all crazy-mixed and not perform at all. Or anyway, not just then and there.

Some puppies sleep all night long and do not need to be taken out until 8 a.m., whilst others are deplorable night birds, and seem, to their harassed owners, to spend the hours of darkness in spending pennies, or worse. There is no point in getting cross or fussed about this, as they do eventually grow up and conform to custom.

The great secrets of puppy training are watchfulness, regularity, patience, quietness and gentleness, and love and understanding.

Just as bed-wetting in children can be caused by bad day-time management—over-stimulation, lack of rest, dietetic deficiencies (frequently lack of calcium and Vitamin B or a correct calcium-phosphorus balance) or psychological troubles, so it is with puppies (and fear of unjust punishment can be a very common cause as this creates a vicious circle). If your puppy after the age of five months is persistently dirty, it would be as well to check on his diet, his health, and his treatment.

Young puppies need just as much sleep and rest as babies and small children, and although most puppies are good at alternating their periods of play with periods of sleep and relaxation, they do occasionally need careful supervision over this—especially if they are brought up in a household of children and other dogs. Every puppy should have his own box or basket—although I prefer a box until after teething is over as they are all too apt to chew their baskets to bits—where he can retire in absolute privacy when he so feels inclined.

Children can be little devils with puppies, never leaving them alone for one moment. So can visitors. ('Oh! The sweet little poppet! *Do* let me hold him. Look George! Isn't it *sweet?*'—and the poor pup gets yanked out of the first decent rest he has managed to get that day.) You would not allow your visitors to waken your baby, so be equally firm over your puppy. Let him get all the rest and sleep his growing body requires, and remember that a puppy has to grow as much in twelve months as a human being does in eighteen years.

Teach your young and visitors how to lift a puppy properly too, which is by supporting it under the body, and not by the scruff of the neck or by one leg. Some people too have a harmful habit of holding a puppy so that its elbows are sticking out, which will not help its front action later. They are on a par with those stupid adults who lead a child along by the hand, well above its head, so that its shoulder is almost dislocated. And, in my opinion, they need to be taught better.

Teasing a puppy is another unforgivable sin, and children are not the only culprits. All good puppies are born with an innate urge to please their owners, and they do try to understand what is said to them. (Watch any dog when you talk to it.) If you tease it, or allow others to tease it, it may be very funny at the time—if you *like* cheap jokes at others' expense, that is—but it can cause endless trouble later, as the poor puppy gets all crazy-mixed, and doesn't know what to believe or do.

Firmness and consistency are two other very essential factors in house-training. It is now years and years and years since I learnt better, through trial and error, than to smack a puppy—even with a rolled-up newspaper, but I never give an order now, either to a child or a puppy, without patiently and firmly seeing that it is carried out. I have also learnt to reduce my orders to the absolute minimum, and so reduce the chance of nagging or fussing.

I also stick to the same phraseology: '*Heel!*' '*Sit!*' '*Stay!*' '*Leave!*' and '*No!*' being the main words to begin with.

I also praise and pet them when they do what they are told. I also never use the dog's pet name when I am cross, as I believe in keeping that name for happy associations.

I do not give any of my dogs tit-bits at meal times, and I don't allow other people to do so either. In fact, I train my adult Bull-mastiffs to refuse food from strangers, and unless a dog is very difficult to train to obedience work, I don't use food as a bribe.

Food, in my opinion, should be kept for eating at the correct regular times.

Jack Russells, on the whole, and if properly fed, are not thieves, but it is as well to watch a puppy, especially with a loaded tea trolley, and say firmly '*Leave!*' if he shows signs of becoming too interested.

And if you do not want him to jump on your clean glazed chintz make this perfectly clear from the beginning: don't let him do it sometimes and not others, and come to a working agreement with the rest of the family over this, as, if he is allowed to do it when you are not there, he won't understand why he mustn't when you *are* there. Also, don't let him do it when the covers are dirty and don't matter, but not when they are clean, as his brain cannot distinguish between these subtleties.

Car-training should be begun as young as possible, with short journeys to the shops. Don't leave him alone in the car for more than a few minutes at first, and always reassure him that you are coming back soon. I have two orders for my dogs when I leave the car—'*Stay!*' when I am leaving them for some time (e.g. while I am in church, or having lunch with a friend) and 'Good dogs—I'll be back soon!' for a short period, such as popping into the post-office or into the fishmonger's.

Lead training is sometimes tricky, as the puppy may buck and kick like a bronco at first, but the earlier you start the easier it is. Never, however, drag a reluctant puppy along on its belly with all four feet digging into the earth in protest. Turn it into a game, and let the puppy lead you at first all round the garden, and don't continue the first few lessons for too long at a time. Five minutes is quite long enough— gradually increasing as it gets accustomed to the idea.

I was once nearly beaten by a Boston Terrier, who resisted all my efforts for weeks, until one night I took him in the car to Edinburgh to see two of our boys off on the night train back to school after the holidays. The station was crowded, noisy, and rather alarming for a small dog, so I slipped his collar and lead over his head and tucked him under my arm to take him to the platform for the final farewells. However, he was heavy, and I was burdened with bags, so, almost without thinking, I put him down. Much to my surprise, he led like a lamb (a particularly silly metaphor, incidentally, as lambs are far from easy to lead). And from that time on I never had any more trouble with him. I suppose that at long last he suddenly saw the point of the exercise, and the necessity of the lead, and it gave him reassurance. Since then I have tried the station, or other crowded place, method with great success on other recalcitrant leaders.

Actually, unless a puppy is a confirmed bolter, it is far better only to use the lead when you really have to—in crowded streets, or when going to ground or working with ferrets, or when giving other dogs a chance at rats, and then not for long.

Puppies should also be trained not to jump up on people. Some don't mind, but others do, and terriers generally have muddy paws. This is a fairly simple matter of saying 'Down!' whenever they do it, although sometimes it is also necessary to add 'Sit!' and make them do that, by pressing on their hindquarters at the same time as you raise their heads by pushing upwards from their throats. Sitting is then automatic, until in time only a slight pressure on their hindquarters is necessary, and thereafter only the command.

Swift and automatic obedience to the command *'Sit!'* has frequently saved lives, especially in towns, when the dog has suddenly seen something on the other side of the road that it wants to investigate, and it is not on a lead.

I used also to train my terriers not to bolt into the house the moment they returned from a muddy country walk, but

All puppies are enchanting, and Jack Russells are no exception. But before you succumb to the appealing look, think carefully about the commitment that buying a dog, any dog, means. And don't be deceived by the Jack Russell's small size, they are extremely active and need plenty of exercise.

to wait in the hall or back kitchen until their feet were dried, and they were rubbed down with a towel or old newspaper, and the effort expended in so training them was well worth the effort saved in housework. They learn very quickly— especially if there are older, well-trained dogs with them to set a good example.

In fact, example is the easiest way to train puppies, either outside or in, and once you have an older dog or two to act as models, your puppy-training efforts will be surprisingly lightened. A well-trained mum is invaluable.

Chapter 7

PRO AND CON THE KENNEL CLUB

At the present time there is a deep and wide abyss between two schools of opinion, with a few odd characters like myself balanced precariously on a tight-rope bridge between them.

On the one side, in a minority as yet, are those who would like to join the Kennel Club, have a properly drawn-up breed standard officially recognised, register their dogs, and keep authentically endorsed pedigrees, run classes for Jack Russells at the bigger shows, with, eventually, challenge certificates on offer, with judges chosen from an approved breed list to award them.

On the other side, in the majority, are those who say firmly and emphatically, 'Not on your life! Just look what has happened to the Bedlington, to the Sealyham, to the Lakeland, to the Welsh, to the Airedale, to the Scottie, to the Skye, and above all, to the Fox Terrier since the Kennel Club got them into its clutches! No—we're keeping the Jack Russell to ourselves, and the way it is.'

At the moment, the Jack Russell Terrier occupies a truly unique position of being one of the most popular breeds in this country (and others—as Jack Russells are now being exported all over the world) while still remaining outside the official pale.

And this state of affairs, in the long run, could be worse for the breed than joining the Kennel Club.

In the good old days, Jack Russells were kept and bred mainly for working purposes. Litters were only bred from proved and tried parents of indubitable courage and stamina, and a puppy that was nervous or timid had short shrift. Now breeding kennels are springing up all over the place; Jack Russells are widely advertised in the dog papers, the sporting press, *The Times, Daily Telegraph* and others, as pets as well as for work. The general public is beginning to buy them as pets, and prices are rising from the original fiver to quite large sums. In other words, the rot has already begun to set in.

The Rev. Jack Russell kept careful pedigrees of all his dogs, and a lot of breeders are following his example. In almost every case, I am convinced, those pedigrees are genuine and authentic, and the breeders reliable and sincere. But—as the craze for keeping Jack Russells as pets spreads, will this happy state of affairs last? Or will some less reliable characters start to jump on the band-waggon? Would it not be safer to register all good dogs, so that each pedigree can be authentically guaranteed and checked? I am well aware that the opposite school of thought does not really believe in pedigrees, but prefers to breed from tried and trusted and true dogs who have proved their integrity and worth—and let me say that I am in entire agreement with this excellent policy—*if* it is always carried out. But in my early days of searching for a good Jack Russell, I was offered all sorts of very dubious dogs that were not my idea of a Jack Russell at all, although their breeders obviously thought they were. And I am by no means the only person who has found this.

Incidentally, it is not the much-maligned Kennel Club that ruins so many working breeds—it is the breeders themselves. All the Kennel Club does is to sponsor Breed Clubs, and ensure that their rules are kept. And, in my opinion, their rules are good, and as nearly fool-proof as they can be. As well as controlling the exhibition of show dogs, the Kennel

Club also sponsors Field Trials for gun-dogs, and Obedience Tests for German Shepherds and other breeds, and, curiously enough, an obedience candidate does not necessarily have to be pure-bred.

Moreover, some breeds have survived years of Kennel Club jurisdiction and exhibition without in any way losing their original form and characteristics. The Border Terrier for one. Yet almost every good Border in the country is registered, and so have his ancestors been for years back. Classes for Border Terriers are scheduled at almost every championship show, and at most of the others. Competition is good and keen, and more champions are made every year. Registrations are still rising. The fact that the essential qualities of the Border Terrier remain unchanged is largely due to the enthusiasm and keenness of their breeders, and to the watchful vigilance of the Breed Club and its committee.

The Cairn Terrier is another very old-established breed that has been registered with the Kennel Club for years, and which still retains all its old vitality, shape, form, and characteristics. So, up to a point, is the Staffordshire Bull Terrier—another very old-established breed. So has the Manchester—which although in the doldrums for a number of years is now enjoying a revival, and is once more back on the map. The Australian and Norwich Terriers are comparative newcomers to the show ring, but they, too, seem to be holding their own without any noticeable deterioration.

In other breeds, to mention only a few, Salukis, Deerhounds, Irish Wolfhounds, Basset Hounds, Bull-mastiffs, Labradors, Springer Spaniels, Weimeraners, Rottweilers, German Short-haired Pointers, and many others still retain all their working qualities as well as being show champions or winners. Until recently it was not possible for any gun-dog to qualify as a show champion unless it had also passed its field trial tests, and in Ireland this also applies to terriers as well. Recently the rules applying to gun-dogs have been changed, but a gun-dog still cannot become a full champion until it has qualified in the field as well as the show ring.

Frankly, in my opinion, what ruins a breed is *popularity* and the lure of filthy lucre, but the Breed Clubs are becoming increasingly aware of this, and, to their credit, in these hard times especially, most breeders who have the ultimate good of their chosen breed at heart, are resisting the temptation to make a profit at the expense of the breed as a whole.

The Bulldog was one of the first to suffer, when Bulldogs suddenly shot into the public limelight at the beginning of the century. Actually, the poor Bulldog is in an invidious position, as the original purpose for which it was bred— bull-baiting—has long since died out—but the Bulldog has survived—both as a symbol and a guard.

The Fox Terrier was particularly unfortunate, as it became immensely popular just before the First World War. Good dogs became extremely valuable, changing hands for as much as £1,000. This, of course, meant that no serious breeder or exhibitor was going to risk having a thousand pounds' worth of dog buried in a fall of earth, maimed by a fox or killed by a badger, so they were kept like precious porcelain. And so their working qualities fell into disuse and atrophied— although I know some show dogs that can still give a good account of themselves if given the chance.

The Sealyham rocketed to popularity in between the two Wars, which did not do it any good, to be superseded by the Cocker Spaniel—a much-maligned breed, incidentally, as although I have judged classes of these that I suspected would all bolt like hares if anyone fired a gun, and have known others that were nothing more than fat and pampered lap-dogs, nevertheless there are several strains still going strong and winning the highest honours at shows, who could (and do) stand a long day's work out with the guns, who are a tremendous credit to their breeders.

Incidentally, I also know some Jack Russells who fall

lamentably into the lap-dog class! But that is definitely not their fault. Any dog, and any breed, will deteriorate rapidly if it falls into the wrong hands.

The Kennel Club gets blamed for a lot of sins that are really due to the breeders, and to the inadequate vigilance of the Breed Clubs, and, in my opinion, if one has the real good of any breed at heart, one can do a lot by either joining a club, or forming one, and doing one's utmost to see that the right people are elected to the committee, and stopping any rot that appears to be starting. There are always, of course, the pushers and thrusters who slip on to committees and try to run them for their own ends, but it is surprising how quickly and easily these can be stopped or subdued by a few really honest and sincere and courageous people, who have the moral guts to stand up to them.

Which brings me to a curious phenomenon that I have observed over and over again: people tend to be like their dogs. Not only in some cases in appearance, but in their qualities. Parson Jack Russell, for instance, had all the virtues of his terriers: tremendous stamina, hardihood, a passion for fox-hunting, good sportsmanship, courage, keenness, and intelligence.

I have never been able to decide whether people of certain temperament and qualities naturally gravitate towards certain breeds, or whether certain breeders somehow convey their qualities to their dogs, or whether, more likely, it is a bit of both.

In my own case, I am curiously diffuse about dogs, and have kept and loved a great many different breeds, but my special one is more like my husband than me, so that my particular preference for it is also quite understandable.

All the real Jack Russell addicts I have ever known have been so amazingly like Jack Russells—or their Jack Russells have been so amazingly like them—that I do not honestly think that the breed is at all likely to deteriorate! Not the real hard core, anyway.

Chapter 8

MATING

In the course of a long and largely mis-spent life, I have presided over the nuptials of hundreds of dogs of all breeds—Bull-mastiffs, Basset Hounds, Beagles, Bulldogs, Boston Terriers, Chihuahuas, Maltese, various terriers, gun-dogs, etc., etc.—and the only thing I can truthfully say with my hand on my heart is that *no two matings are ever the same.* Even repeat ones with the same dog and bitch.

Nor, in spite of what the books say, is there any absolutely definite day when the bitch is ready. Some bitches will stand for the dog, and conceive, and have puppies on the sixth day, while others are successfully mated on the twenty-first. I am fully aware that these statements are open to doubt, and I don't really expect anyone to believe me, but I swear they are true. In two of the cases without any possible shadow of doubt, one concerned a Manchester Terrier bitch, who was accidentally mated (luckily by the right dog) on her sixth day. Hoping that it was far too soon for any results, we took her next morning to some boarding kennels, where she stayed for over a month. There was no other Manchester Terrier in the kennels, so that there could not have been a later unobserved mating, yet she whelped five indubitable Manchester pups . . . The other case was a Bull-mastiff bitch, who was carefully kept in purdah until her twenty-first day, when all seemed well, so she was returned to her run, which she shared with a young dog (also, of course, a Bull-mastiff). Nine weeks to the day later, she whelped, to our great surprise, as she had shown no signs of being pregnant, two very fine Bull-mastiff puppies. There have been other cases, where I am fairly certain that the bitch has conceived well outside the usual time, but none that I can be as absolutely sure about as these. I mean, accidents can, and often do, happen and bitches on heat can be cunning.

However, a rough guide is that from the twelfth to the fifteenth day after the heat commences, the discharge stops, and the bitch indicates her willingness to stand for the dog by twisting her tail to one side. Some bitches have quite a long period of potential fertility, lasting for about a week, while others have to be caught at the psychological moment. On the whole, with a keen stud dog, I would rather have a bitch who is just past it, than one who is not quite ready, as in the latter case she will not stand willingly. In the former, she will, but the dog very often won't play.

Jack Russell bitches, in my experience, are incorrigible flirts, but frequently extremely choosy about their mates— often showing an unaccountable preference for the most unsuitable ones, such as the collie down the road, or the Labrador up the way, or indeed anything except their chosen Jack Russell mate.

The heat first shows its advent by a slight swelling of the vulva, followed, in a few days, by a discharge, which gradually becomes more profuse, and turns into blood. Bitches vary a great deal, and some, especially young ones, hardly show anything at all. About the twelfth day onwards this discharge stops, and it is then, and not before, that the bitch is ready. This highly fertile period can last for only a few hours, in some cases, up till over a week, when the vulva gradually returns to normal.

A bitch should most definitely not be mated until she is fully mature, and this is not until the second heat, and sometimes the third, depending upon how old she was when her first heat began. Some bitches start at six months—while others are eleven months or a year. Although I have heard of some cases who were eighteen months, I have also suspected that the first heat may have passed unnoticed.

I personally do not believe in breeding from any bitch more than once a year, but some breeders do it twice running, and then rest the bitch for a year before her next litter without, apparently, doing her any harm. However, nursing a litter does take a lot out of a bitch, and she takes some time to build up her reserves again.

I am a great believer in natural matings, by which I mean letting the dog and the bitch get to know each other, and play together for a while first. Quite often, the bitch will be unwilling to begin with, but, given time and patience, she generally accepts the dog if left to herself. Some stud dogs, however, are over-keen, and in this case supervision, with the dog on a lead, is necessary. Also some dogs are far too ardent and impetuous, and inclined to shoot their bolt too soon. In which case, he has to be rested before trying again, with the bitch right away and out of sight.

After the mating is accomplished, there is usually a 'tie', with the two animals firmly locked together. Supervision is necessary here, as the bitch may try to pull away, or sit down, or even roll over, which may hurt the dog badly, so it is necessary to hold her and reassure her. Some unproved dogs also get a bit worried, and need reassurance, but not as a general rule.

(Never shall I forget a mating between two virgin Basset Hounds, both about a yard long, in our drawing-room with Wagner's 'Ride of the Valkyrie' going full blast on the record-player. I rashly left them both together to make friends, never expecting that they would consummate their nuptials quite so soon. My husband, hearing the most dreadful din, rushed into the room to see what on earth was happening, to find me kneeling in helpless laughter on the floor, vainly trying to reach both their heads, the Basset Hounds giving indignant tongue at the tops of their voices, and a full orchestra knocking hell out of the Valkyrie.)

Incidentally, it is a good idea to make sure that the bitch relieves herself before being introduced to the dog. And if she has travelled a long way, has a rest and drink, and time to get accustomed to her strange surroundings. It is even better, if possible, to take the dog to the bitch.

In some cases, with a maiden bitch, it may be necessary to stretch the vagina by hand first. This can be helped with Vaseline, but do *not* overdo the Dettol or disinfectant when you wash your hands as a preliminary, or you may put the dog right off—as I did once. They don't like disinfectant— and indeed it can be used as a deterrent if you do not want to mate your bitch and wish to keep off suitors—only be careful not to apply it too strong or you'll burn her.

Other deterrents are Amplex (given orally in tablets every four hours), TCP, or various sprays which are on the market, and which your veterinary surgeon will recommend. It is a good idea to spray anywhere the bitch is likely to have left her scent. There is now a canine contraceptive pill, but I should get your own veterinary surgeon's advice before using it on your bitch.

After the mating, the bitch should be left as quietly as possible, and encouraged to rest. Some people like two matings, but I have never found this necessary.

Although a tie is the normal thing, I have had several matings, especially with Chihuahuas, where a perfectly fertile mating has occurred without this.

Natural matings are the best, but if the bitch is particularly obstreperous, and just will not stand, or keeps attacking the dog, and if you are perfectly certain this is not because she is not ready, but just being awkward, then you can muzzle her with a bandage, passed round her muzzle, crossed beneath it and tied behind her neck. But I have never yet found this necessary. It is also sometimes necessary, with a bitch that will keep on sitting down at the critical moment, to pass your hand under her loins and support her, at the same time talking to her gently and reassuring her. This reassuring of maiden bitches really is important, as a lot can be achieved by voice alone.

Arabella, bitch puppy of Bumble, at two weeks old. Her ears have dropped and eyes opened. The Jack Russell's typical wide digging paws are already evident.

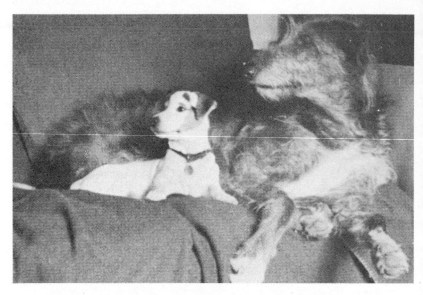

Above Arabella at three months on the sofa with Louisa, her new
owner's Deerhound.

Below Arabella learns to sit and also to tolerate a collar.

Arabella is meant to be retrieving this old shoe, but in the typically nosy way of terriers suspects there may be something lurking in the toe.

Arabella decides to pick up the shoe and bring it to her mistress, but not without running round in circles with it first! Terriers can be taught to retrieve, but it is not their natural job and so requires much time and patience on the owner's part.

There *is* chocolate in the bottom of this boot. Arabella proves she has a nose!

Above Arabella at seven weeks.
Below Arabella returns to visit her mother, Bumble. They took quite a little while to settle down, the bond between them very clearly having been broken.

Chapter 9

WHELPING

During the years I have been breeding dogs, and these include terriers, toys, gun-dogs, hounds, bull-breeds and the odd accidental cross-bred litter, I have only twice needed the assistance of a veterinary surgeon, although I must have whelped over one hundred litters by now.

On the first occasion he got stuck in a snow-drift and never arrived at all, so I had to boil the sugar-tongs and perform a Milne-Murray high forceps delivery on my own, after anaesthetising the Bulldog bitch with some ether, which I kept for removing oil-stains from my husband's trousers. The trouble was due to a most unusual complication of Siamese twins—joined at the navel, but I managed to save all the puppies, bar one of the twins, who had to be sacrificed to save the other. The bitch, once she had recovered from the anaesthetic, was none the worse.

On the other occasion—a Bull-mastiff this time—the bitch developed leukaemia during her pregnancy. We lost all the puppies, but the bitch survived, although, of course, her life-span was soon after ended by this dread disease.

I must confess that I once panicked when one of my bitches had not produced her first puppy four hours after starting labour, but my vet just laughed at me—and sure enough, the moment he was out of the house, she whelped with ease.

I am glad to be able to relate that, with those three

exceptions, all my bitches have appeared to enjoy whelping and, apart from some restlessness and panting, have never shown any signs of distress.

As this happy state of affairs cannot all be entirely due to luck, I think that my three great secrets are:

(a) I have never bred from a bitch without a good temperament
(b) I have never bred from a bitch without a good pelvic formation
(c) I have allowed all my bitches, within reason, to whelp where and how they wanted to.

Contrary to the opinion of several people, I have never thought that the size of the bitch matters—provided (and this is all-important) that her pelvic formation is correct, and wide enough to allow an easy passage for the puppies.

Correct pelvic formation can be gauged fairly accurately by watching the bitch's hind action, which is controlled from the pelvis, and if she moves well, and is wide across the loin, then all is generally well. I also always feel the pelvic bones and hip-joints, and if these are set wide and at a good angle, then all is well too—although the two things are interdependent, and I have found that it is possible to assess the hind action before the bitch ever moves, from the conformation of the pelvis.

Of course, one occasionally gets the odd puppy coming the wrong way round, or feet first, or with a very large head, but these can generally be gently assisted by manipulation in between spasms.

As regards size not mattering, I had adequate proof of this on one particular occasion when a really tiny Chihuahua bitch (weighing under three pounds) went off the rails with a fifteen-pound Boston dog. By the time we realised that the Worst Had Happened, it was far too late to do anything about it. However, I arranged for her to have a Caesarian section, just in case. She beat me and the vet to it by about four days, and whelped two very handsome dog pups *in my bed* with no bother at all—except to me, who had to clean up.

Jack Russells, on the whole, whelp very easily, as the puppies have small heads. Also as they seldom have large litters (four or five being about the average) there are no complications due to inside congestion and traffic jams as the puppies begin to move down the tunnel.

Pre-natal care is a good thing, as long as you don't overdo it. Some people fuss too much—over-feed their bitch, and cut down her exercise too much—and treat her too like precious porcelain. While I should not advocate a hard day's hunting, or running for miles behind a horse, normal exercise is good for them—only be careful not to let her jump down off things, or clear a wall or a fence during the last few weeks.

Few bitches will want to, but some get so excited when a hare or a rabbit gets up in front of them that they throw caution to the winds. However, a terrier of mine once chased (to my impotent horror) a hare right across a ploughed field and scrambled over a high stone wall, dropping heavily down on the far side, just a week before she whelped four puppies, so they are tougher than one might imagine.

I cut down their carbohydrates (terrier meal, etc.) while they are pregnant and increase their raw meat ration to compensate. I also give them an additional meal of fresh milk and eggs in the morning. I also give them a daily dose of vitamin tablets, if I think they need conditioning. Worming *before* they are mated, is sometimes a good idea, if you suspect the presence of worms, but I don't like it after they are definitely pregnant.

As D-day draws near, I bring out the box I fondly hope they will whelp in. This is always disinfected and dried in the sun (if the sun obliges) both after the last litter, and some time before the next. Do not, on any account, scrub it out at the last minute and let the bitch lie in a damp box stinking of Dettol (which they *hate*). I know that you personally would never be so silly—but you'd be surprised at how silly other people are!

If the bitch is small, a grocer's cardboard box makes the ideal indoor whelping bed. I cut out one of the sides, not quite to the bottom, which keeps it draught-proof. Some bitches—Chihuahuas especially—like the lid left on, so that they are in a little enclosed kennel, but terriers and Bostons seem to prefer it open at the top.

Some bitches prefer absolute privacy—especially if they have had a litter before. Others like you to stand by and reassure them. Your bitch will, no doubt, let you know which category she belongs to.

House or kennel is another problem. If your bitch is accustomed to kennel life and regularly sleeps outside, then she will want to whelp in her kennel, and you will only upset her if you try to bring her indoors at the last moment. Be sure, however, that it is warm and dry, and that her whelping box is raised off the ground. I always use newspapers as bedding during whelping, as they are warm, easily changed and burnt, and she can tear it up to make a nest if she wants. Straw is all very well, but it is often dirty, and has nasty sharp stalks that can damage a puppy's eyes. Also, it sticks to the bitch sometimes after parturition. Peat moss, they say, is good, but I have never tried it myself. You'll need piles and piles of newspapers before the puppies are all weaned and away, so start collecting the moment your bitch is served. Keep them if you can, in a dust-proof cupboard, so that they are fresh and clean for the occasion.

Equally, a bitch that is normally kept in the house should not be banished to a kennel to whelp. This would be stupid and cruel.

As her hour approaches, the bitch will indicate this by an increased swelling of the vulva, and sometimes a small discharge.

She will either become restless, and tend to follow you around like a shadow, or she will go quietly off to her box and get on with the job by herself. Kennel bitches vary—but on the whole they prefer to be left alone. Keep an unostentatious eye on even these, however, as complications can occur. Or a puppy can get left out in the cold and die.

Some house-dogs will reject their accustomed box, or the one carefully prepared for them, and wander around looking for all sorts of likely and unlikely places. On the whole, terriers are good and sensible, but Chihuahuas can be the end over this.

And I once had a Bulldog which insisted on whelping in my husband's favourite armchair. I simply tucked a mackintosh sheet well into all the corners, covered it with thick brown paper, and covered that with newspaper, and let her get on with it. Once the puppies were born (nine of them), she was quite willing to let me move them and her to more suitable quarters.

The great thing, with a bitch of this type, I think, is reassurance. So I generally sit nearby, with my typewriter or my knitting and a book, and say at intervals, '*Clever* girl! Clever Tosca! Having puppies, love? That's fine!' or some such asinine remarks. I don't go near her unless she wants me to particularly. Sometimes a puppy has to be eased out. If this is necessary, never pull or tug—but simply wait for the next push—and then draw it gently forwards and downwards. If a paw has got forward or the pup is in an awkward position, it is often possible to remedy this in between spasms. (Wash and disinfect your hands first, of course.) The great secret is to do everything slowly and gently, talking to the bitch meanwhile.

Generally, the bitch herself will clean her puppies, and

deal with the cord and afterbirth. (And don't stop her from eating this—as it is nature's way of supplying her with iron and other elements.) But if she doesn't, then make sure that the puppy can breathe all right, and has not got a caul over its head. You may also have to cut the cord (with sterilised surgical scissors, please). She will lick it dry herself, so that there is no need to tie bits of thread around it.

After the second puppy is born, it is sometimes necessary to keep a watchful eye on the first, in case it gets lain on or cast aside and chilled. Puppies must have warmth—and will die if they don't get it. Sixty-five to seventy degrees Fahrenheit is about right for terriers. In cold weather an infra-red lamp (as for pigs) is useful, but don't put it too near the bitch or she will get too hot and start panting.

If a puppy is born apparently dead, it can often be revived by breathing down its throat and working its tiny rib-cage gently and rhythmically with your hands. A drop or two of brandy and warm milk, from an eye-dropper, is also a handy restorative.

Before you leave the bitch, make sure that she has enough milk to feed them. Sometimes, especially with a first litter, it does not come immediately, but the puppies should be all right for a few hours, and their suckling helps to bring it on.

Some puppies squeal at birth and continue to squeak and squeal for a few hours, but a really well-fed and healthy litter should be silent. If they are still squealing next morning, they are probably hungry, and may need some supplementary feeding. Or a puppy may squeal because it has got lost and cannot find its way back to the milk bar. Most bitches can deal with this themselves, but inexperienced young mums sometimes need a nursery maid. Anyway, if you hear a puppy squealing twenty-four hours after birth—*go and see what is wrong*. You may save its life.

The bitch will probably refuse food at first, but she will be grateful for a drink—either of water or warm milk and honey. Take her out (you'll probably have to carry her) to relieve herself after it is all over, and again at regular intervals.

Don't worry if her motions are black, or if she is still bleeding a little. That will clear up within a week. If not call your vet.

See that she has clean water always available, and clean dry bedding. And the best of luck to you!

Chapter 10

WHELPING COMPLICATIONS

The most likely whelping complications to affect Jack Russell bitches are: (a) a wrongly-positioned puppy, (b) insufficient milk or 'hefted' milk, (c) uterine inertia, (d) restlessness, (e) eclampsia.

(a) A wrongly presented puppy can often be manipulated into the right position by yourself, but if this proves too difficult, send for your vet at once, as it may mean a Caesarian section.

(b) Insufficient milk should eventually improve with suckling, but sometimes the two back teats become engorged and swollen—with no milk coming through to the other teats. In this case, you can help by fomenting the affected nipples with hot cloths, and drawing off the milk by hand. This milk is often 'hefted', i.e. too thick and stale for the puppies, but if it is drawn off once or twice it should come in all right. Never let your bitch remain with engorged teats, as they are very painful—and it may also put her off her puppies.

(c) Uterine inertia is rare in terriers, but can occur, and if the first puppy has not put in an appearance within about five hours of the commencement of labour (i.e. when the bitch begins to strain) send for the vet. It may be a stuck puppy, or she may need an injection of pituitrin to help things on. But never allow any bitch to strain and strain ineffectually for too long.

Another danger signal is too long an interval between puppies. An hour and a half, in my opinion, is quite long enough (and they should appear at twenty-minute or half-hour intervals if all is going well).There may, however, be a lull between the two branches of the uterus. The canine womb is Y-shaped, and generally carries half the litter in each side. After the first arm is emptied, there may well be a hiatus of over an hour during which nothing happens. In this case, the bitch settles down happily to lick and nurse the first contingent, and appears contented until the next pains begin. If, however, she continues to strain during this time, or looks anxious, then it is as well to send for the vet.

(d) Restlessness. Most bitches are restless before they settle down to labour, but if this continues after birth, she needs watching, as it could be due to a calcium deficiency and the forerunner of eclampsia. Milk and honey is good, and so are calcium tablets, and she may settle down all right after her appetite returns and she is functioning normally again.

(e) Eclampsia. This is a terrifying thing—which sometimes occurs during the third week of lactation. The bitch will stagger, and fall, and often lose consciousness. The remedy is to get her as soon as possible (as even minutes are precious) to your vet for a calcium injection—after which the bitch returns to normal remarkably quickly and appears to be none the worse. Nevertheless, if the vet advises you to wean the puppies immediately, you would be wise to take his advice. Ever since one of my Chihuahuas nearly died of this, while nursing a litter of six, I have kept a syringe and some calcium borogluconate on the premises—just in case.

Chapter 11

BRINGING UP THE BABIES

For the first three or four weeks of their lives all that the puppies need is warmth, sleep and their mother's milk. The dam will keep them clean by licking them. This licking also stimulates their excretory functions, enabling them to pass urine and stools. These stools, incidentally, will be almost black for the first day or two, but this is perfectly normal.

DOCKING
If you are going to dock your puppies' tails it *must* be done before they are a week old. It is quite simple to do and at this early age no anaesthetic is necessary, but if you are a novice it is better to get the help of an expert or your veterinary surgeon. A pair of *sharp* surgical scissors, or a *sharp* knife, some lint and a styptic pencil are all that you need.

Remove each puppy separately, and take it well away from the bitch, and out of earshot, as they sometimes squeal and this would upset her. Cut the puppy's tail to the required length but if in doubt it is better for the tail to be longer than shorter. The expert eye knows where to cut—between the caudal vertibrae. Pull the skin over the stump, after using the styptic pencil, and return the puppy quickly to the dam, who will do the rest by licking. Try to do this job as quietly and unfussily and as matter-of-factly as possible in order not to

Note the length of this Jack Russell's tail. It is exactly right and
gives the dog a well-balanced look.

upset the mother unduly. Bitches are very quick to sense any
nervousness, and react accordingly, but if the owner remains
calm and serene, so will the bitch. Ask your vet to do the job
if you feel squeamish.

For the first ten days, the puppies' eyes are tightly shut,
and they are also deaf, nuzzling their way to the milk bar
and the warmth of their dam's side, by smell and instinct, so
that they do not feel much or get upset by being treated so
inhumanely.

Some people disapprove of tail docking, preferring to leave
the tail at its natural length. This is largely a matter of

opinion, but if you intend to work your terriers docked tails are less likely to be trapped and injured.

CLAWS

Another thing to watch is that their tiny, needle-sharp claws do not grow too long and scratch the dam while they scrabble at the milk-bar. They can inflict quite painful scratches that can turn into sores—and as they grow older and begin to climb over each other and play, they can also scratch each other quite badly. Until they begin to run about, and so keep their claws worn down by exercise, they need to be trimmed about once a week. Be very careful not to snip below the quick, or you will hurt them and make them bleed. You can see the quick quite clearly, as the nails are transparent.

The navel cords should have shrivelled up and dropped off within the first few days after birth, but it is as well to examine each puppy carefully for any signs of navel hernia or sores which may need attention.

MILK

Also be certain that the bitch has enough milk—especially if it is her first litter. The fact that the puppies all appear to be sucking does not necessarily mean that they are all getting fed adequately. Some bitches are slow to lactate, although the sucking is the best stimulant for this. Others, generally due to malnutrition during pregnancy, just do not have enough milk, and so supplementary feeding may be necessary from the very start. The best way to tell if this is required is by the behaviour and appearance of the puppies themselves. If they are as fat as little butter-balls, with their tiny tums full, silent, and asleep most of the time, then all is well, but if they are restless and continually squealing plaintively, then some supplementary feeding is essential—either for a day or two until the bitch's milk flows in, or for all the time.

Bitch's milk has a much higher fat and protein content than

cow's milk—and a higher protein content than goat's milk, so that these need to be supplemented. Probably the easiest way is to mix a tablespoon of full cream dried milk to a half-pint of cow's milk. Heat the milk to boiling point, but don't let it boil, and then add it slowly, stirring all the time and smoothing out the lumps, to the dried milk in a bowl, and give it to the puppies either in a grapefruit spoon, an eye-dropper, or (later) a premature baby's bottle, at blood heat, which for dogs is about 100 degrees Fahrenheit. See that it is going down their tiny throats and not coming down through their noses or choking them. If milk does come continually down a puppy's nose, it may have a cleft palate—although this is rare in Jack Russells. In this case ask your vet's advice, but in my opinion it is better to put the puppy down.

HUMANE KILLING
Jack Russells are generally born sound and healthy, but very occasionally malformed puppies are born. If you are so unlucky, get the vet to inject a lethal dose of drug.

WEANING
At about ten days old the puppies open their eyes and begin to crawl about. Within a few more days they are up on their legs and staggering unsteadily around, exploring every inch of their box, and becoming venturesome. Occasionally one manages to clamber over the edge and fall outside and is unable to climb back. He will probably let everyone know about this at the top of his voice, and his mum will generally rescue him. Nevertheless *never* hear a puppy squeal for more than a few seconds without investigating, as they can so easily become chilled and die during those first few vital weeks. They can also get round behind the dam, and squashed between her and the wall of the box, or lain on, although, on the whole, Jack Russells are clever mothers, and look after their puppies well.

About the fourth week, introduce shallow saucers of fortified warm milk, and see if the puppies will learn to lap. Let the bitch lap too, if she wants to, as this will show them how, and the milk she drinks will do her good. There will be a certain amount of overbalancing head-first into the saucer to begin with, and a great deal of spluttering and puffing and blowing, but they soon get the hang of it all and begin to lap like old stagers.

If the bitch and her litter are still indoors, at this stage, it is a good idea to make a run for them that allows the bitch to escape if she wants to, whilst still keeping the puppies within bounds. A children's play-pen, reinforced with netting nailed round the base so that they cannot slip through the rails, will do, but do cut a bit down at one side to let the bitch jump out if she wants to, and get away from her importunate family. If they are in an outside kennel (and if they are, this *must* be kept warm—over sixty-five degrees Fahrenheit for the first few weeks) give her a raised bench for a bed that the puppies cannot get up on to. If the bitch never gets any peace, she will sometimes turn on her puppies quite savagely at this stage, and, although she never means to hurt them badly, she can kill them accidentally, as Jack Russells have strong jaws and sharp teeth.

I generally introduce supplementary feeding at about the fourth week, gradually increasing this, but I let the bitch and puppies wean themselves, either by mutual consent, or by the gradual disappearance of the puppies, one by one, to their new homes. I leave the one I am keeping with its dam, especially at night, until they part of their own accord.

I also find that the dam is by far the best teacher, when the puppy reaches the age of being trained for sport. She will also, if she is a well-trained house dog, teach her puppy to be clean and well-behaved indoors, which will save you a lot of bother.

In fact, all my bitches have been perfectly sweet with their puppies, and most apologetic if an accident does happen! They will also generally clean it up themselves, if it does, leaving only the final rinse to me.

Incidentally, if an accident should occur on your best pale green Wilton carpet, by far the best thing to do, if the mother is absent, is to squirt a jet of soda-water on the spot, as the alkali in the soda counteracts the uric acid, and prevents staining. I have managed successfully to combine puppies and fitted carpets for years now.

As long as the puppies are still on a milk diet, there is very little acid in their urine, but after meat is introduced things are different.

Raw scraped meat should be gradually added to their diet from the age of four weeks onwards—just about a thumb-nail-sized quantity at first, until they are getting about a tablespoonful. After eight weeks this can be minced or chopped. Do remember that the great secret of rearing a healthy litter and avoiding tummy upsets is to introduce each new food gradually, in very small amounts to begin with. Chapter 12 deals with feeding puppies in more detail.

WORMING

For some reason that I have never been able to understand or prevent, in spite of the many methods advocated by the herb school of theorists and others, *all* puppies are infested with roundworms. I will deal more fully with those horrible parasites in Chapter 17, but all that I want to impress upon the novice breeder here and now is that *worming is necessary*. Although there are a great many proprietary remedies sold over the counter, I always ask the veterinary surgeon for his own prescription, and follow his instructions implicitly, and I do most strongly advise you to do the same. Fasting before dosing is now utterly unnecessary, and in my experience puppies can be effectively wormed without being upset by it in the very slightest.

It is advisable to worm twice, the second time about ten days after the first, but be absolutely certain that each pill is safely down each individual puppy. It is extremely exasperating to find a disgorged worm pill on the kennel floor ten minutes later, without having a clue about which puppy is the culprit! They can be administered in warm milk (pulverised first), or in butter or a pellet of scraped raw meat, but I find it easiest just to pop the pills over the puppies' throats, and then hold their mouths shut, and stroke their throats gently until they swallow once or twice. Even then they have to be watched in case they regurgitate. But worms can be so debilitating and such a pest that it is well worth taking a little extra trouble, and to mak' siccar. Some puppies are adept at either holding the pill back or sicking it up after it goes down, so that it is advisable to worm each puppy well away from its brethren, and to keep it apart for a while, until you are convinced that all is well and the pill absorbed. In this way, you can be sure that no puppy has been dosed twice, and one missed.

Tapeworms are most rare in young puppies, although a pest in older dogs, but I shall deal with them later.

Jack Russell puppies are terrors for chewing and swallowing foreign objects. Luckily nature has made provision for this, and they generally pass them within forty-eight hours, without undue distress, but if you suspect any obstruction, or if the puppy strains at stool, keeps retching, or passes blood or has diarrhoea then get the vet at once. An X-ray may be necessary and even an operation. I once lost a most promising young puppy who swallowed the works of a toy car which one of my own young had left lying around on the floor.

On the other hand, I once had a terrier puppy who swallowed and successfully passed through its intestines a bottle top off a ginger ale. And another who produced over a yard of string.

INOCULATION (see also page 99)

All puppies should be inoculated against distemper, hard-pad, leptospiral jaundice and parvovirus disease. This is expensive, but well worth the money, and an excellent investment. Some vets will not do this until the puppy is over three months old, while others believe in doing it before they leave the nest. Both theories seem to be effective—as I have never known a puppy contract either disease before weaning—whilst my early-inoculated puppies have proved just as immune as the later ones. One summer, we had a devastating outbreak of hard-pad all around us, including deaths of dogs that had actually been on our premises and playing with my own dogs during what must have been their infectious period. Some of our dogs had been inoculated before three months old, while we were still in Scotland, and before we moved to Herefordshire, whilst others had been done later, as my present vet belongs to the after-three-months-old school of thought. I even had one litter that had not been inoculated at all yet as it was still with its mum. Yet none of our dogs was affected. These included Bull-mastiffs, a Boston and several terriers, as well as a couple of Maltese.

I have also had, to my horror, a young dog benched at a show next door to a dog that I was suspicious of at the time, and who developed hard-pad soon afterwards—yet my dog remained immune.

Chapter 12

PUPPY FEEDING

Some bitches regurgitate half-digested food for their puppies. This is not the revolting and disgusting habit it may seem to the uninitiated, but a perfectly natural method of feeding them, and should not be stopped.

At about the fourth week introduce shallow saucers (shallow, because the puppies sometimes overbalance in their excitement and fall in) of fortified milk, gradually increasing the amount until they are getting about half a pint each at eight weeks.

Raw, scraped, clean meat (for human consumption only) should be introduced, very gradually, just about half a teaspoonful at first, at four-five weeks, until they are getting about a quarter of a pound for their main meal at eight weeks and after.

Cod-liver oil may be added to one milk meal, just a few drops, about once a week in summer, and three times a week in winter.

Yolk of egg should be added to the morning milk at about six weeks, again only half an egg to begin with, and only the yolk at first, as the white contains a substance called avidin, which absorbs an important B-group vitamin, called biotin, which is especially necessary for their early health. Later whole eggs can be given, but not until about three months.

These may be whisked into their milk and poured over

their biscuit or porridge. (If porridge is given, it must be thoroughly well cooked, overnight if possible, in a simmering oven.)

Four small meals a day must be given, depending upon how much they are getting still from the bitch, until they are about seven weeks old, when these can be reduced to three larger ones for breakfast, dinner and supper, with perhaps an additional drink of milk and honey at bedtime, before the puppy, if it is in the house, goes out for its last evacuation.

Raw minced meat should by now be its main meal, with breakfast of puppy meal, or porridge, milk and egg; lunch of meat, vegetables and broth, and the main meal at six p.m. of raw meat, puppy meal and milk.

After eight months the meals should be reduced to slightly larger ones of breakfast and supper.

After a year old, unless in whelp, the Jack Russell should have only one meal a day at six p.m.

The meat meal may be varied once or twice a week, with rinsed raw tripe or fish.

Stress (a Vetzyme product) is good for in-whelp and nursing bitches, and growing puppies, as it contains lime and phosphorus, which helps to absorb calcium, which they need for lactation and bone formation.

Chapter 13

FURTHER TRAINING

Adolescent terriers, parted from the benign influence of well-trained, older dogs, can occasionally be troublesome and naughty. As they are bred for hunting, and full of energy and curiosity, they need rather more outlet for these innate urges than the average Bull-breed or Toy dog.

Boredom can become the source of a multitude of sins, ranging from going off hunting on their own (which, if not controlled or diverted, may develop into habitual straying or sheep-worrying), to chewing slippers, hats, books, or anything else they can get hold of.

A large marrow bone is an excellent antidote, but it must be large, and never chicken or rabbit, which may splinter and cause serious, and sometimes fatal, internal damage by perforation and bleeding. It is also useful to provide the puppy with its own special toys, such as a solid rubber ball, or bone, toy mouse, or even a pair of old rolled-up stockings, to keep it amused and occupied.

If your puppy runs away from you, and appears deaf to your word (or yells) of command to come to heel, never make the mistake of running after it or chasing it. Instead, call it, and walk in the opposite direction, when, in most cases, it will run after you. Or stand firmly and call it repeatedly until it returns. Never lose your temper, however exasperating the little so-and-so may be, and always welcome it and praise it for returning.

If you are foolish enough to punish an errant dog when it returns to you, or comes home after playing truant, it will connect the punishment with its return, instead of its truancy, and be far less willing to come home on the next occasion. Restrain yourself to remarking sternly, 'Where have you been?' and then make a fuss of it, and let it know that you still love it.

In extreme cases, a persistent runner-away can be cured by attaching a long length of clothes-line to its collar, then, when it bolts, just before it reaches the end of its tether (and yours) call '*Heel!*' sharply, and jerk the cord, so that it is thrown on its back. But be careful not to dislocate its neck or choke it.

Keep your commands to a minimum, but see that, once given, they are obeyed, even if this means dropping all other urgent jobs for the time being. Given the proverbial inch, terriers will take an ell. And if they are allowed to get away with disobedience once, they will try it on again and again, but are surprisingly sensible, once they realise that you are the master or pack-leader.

Tugging and panting on the lead, while out for a walk, can be an unnecessary nuisance. Check it by a firm jerk and the command '*Heel!*', repeated until the penny drops. I always stop walking, on these occasions, and wait until the lead is slack and the terrier at my heel before continuing the walk. It means somewhat slow progress, at first, but they learn more quickly this way.

A puppy can be taught to sit, at the word of command, by pressing on its hindquarters, and at the same time pressing upwards with the other hand under its chest and throat, meanwhile repeating '*Sit!*'. And, of course, praising it when it complies.

As each new command—'*Heel!*' '*Sit!*' '*Stay!*'—is gradually learnt, one by one, the puppy should be rehearsed in them daily, until they become automatic, but never too often, or it will become bored and sullen. Puppies vary considerably in their speed of learning, and the amount of repetition they can stand, but most of my terriers could absorb one command (repeated twice daily) a week, before going on to the next lesson. Ten minutes at a time is enough.

Chapter 14

A DOG IS A DOG IS A DOG

If you belong to that vast majority of keen Jack Russell owners who live in the country but don't hunt, and have little opportunity of entering their terriers to foxes; if you neither farm yourself, nor know any neighbouring farmer well enough to ask if you may bring your terrier to hunt rats in their steading—or are even afraid of rats—you can still have a tremendous lot more fun on a country walk if you teach your terrier to work intelligently than if you just let him rampage all over the place and chase anything he likes.

Needless to say, never, *never* let him chase sheep, especially in lambing time, or cattle, or horses, or any farm livestock, or you will find yourself the most unpopular dog-owner for miles around. And never let him go off hunting by himself, if you can possibly help it, or he may get himself and you into Big Trouble. Keep him under control, but give him plenty of hard exercise, and allow him to give his hereditary sporting instincts full play, and both you and he will benefit by it.

The British Isles, thank God, are still immensely rich in by-roads and country lanes. Even quite close to motorways it is often possible to find quiet lanes. Most of them, too, are blessed with those deep ditches that are the Jack Russell's happy hunting ground.

The best combination of Jack Russells I know are a well-trained bitch and her young son or daughter, and it is sheer joy to stroll quietly along and watch mum teaching the young entry how to hunt. If you leave them to themselves, only recalling them if, in the excitement of the chase, they get too far ahead of you, or stray from the side of the lane into the fields or woods beyond, you will not only have a wonderful walk, but you will learn the most surprising amount about the wild life that inhabits those hedgerows, ditches, grass verges and banks. You will also discover that your own perceptions are sharpened, and your zest for life keener.

Incidentally, never go out with a Jack Russell without his collar and lead. You can take them off and put them in your pocket, or tie them round your waist, but it is always better to have them with you, not only in case of emergencies, but in case your walk takes you along a road with traffic on it, before you get home. Even the best-trained Jack Russell is all too apt to dart across the road in front of a car or lorry if he sees something exciting on the far side, and it is better to be safe than sorry. They are so incredibly quick too, that they give neither you nor the driver time to think or act, and although my own dogs have been known to disappear right underneath the wheels of a heavy lorry and emerge unscathed at the rear, on two occasions, I am certain that they have shortened my life in the process, as well as that of the poor driver, who drew up, shaking like an aspen leaf, and as white as the proverbial sheet.

But, on the other hand, never allow your dog to *hunt* while wearing a collar: this can all too easily become hanked on a root underground, or catch on a branch, or other obstacle above ground, and your terrier could be choked, or inextricably caught. It is far better to slip the collar and lead off, once one is clear of traffic, and let the terrier run free.

Jack Russells need little encouragement or siccing on—in fact, this is a bad policy as it over-excites them and makes them bark like hyenas at nothing, but they do like their

It will not be so very long before the puppy standing somewhat precariously (*above*) will become the skilful ratter returning with a trophy (*below*).

owners to take an interest in their activities. Every little while they will stop, and look back anxiously, with one paw raised, to see if you are still with them, and even if they are busy clearing a conduit, one at one end and the other at the other, they still occasionally pop out and have a look to see if you are waiting and watching their cleverness. And if they do kill anything, they like you to pick it up and take it home—so that a small sack or gamebag is a useful adjunct, even if your total bag is two dead rats and a weasel. Incidentally, I have found that they are much more willing to break up the party and come home if you carry their bag. Otherwise they are reluctant to leave for hours.

I very often used to carry a small, light spade as well, when I went for a walk with my terriers, and very useful it proved too, on lots of occasions. It was useful to lean against or use as a shooting stick if the ground was too wet and muddy to sit on.

If you only have one Jack Russell, you can still have a lot of fun, but you will have to help him a little more, and also teach him a little. Things like waiting until you get to the other end of a conduit to act as a stop before he plunges in, or looking to see whether there are any other exits from a hollow tree trunk, or a large and inviting hole in a bank, although actually, if you are alone with him, it is not a good idea to let him go to ground, as he may get stuck or lost, and you may not be able to howk him out unaided. And I hate leaving a terrier alone while I go for help, as one can never be sure what he may do in one's absence—from emerging unexpectedly, and, finding himself alone, setting off to look for you and getting lost, to digging himself still further in and getting lost—if he is still young and untrained.

My own policy, with all my various breeds and individual dogs, has been to give them a reasonably free hand to teach me all their inherited lore and wisdom, and I can truthfully say, with my hand on my heart, that I have learnt more from my dogs than from anything or anyone else. Not only that but they have enriched my appreciation and enjoyment of life beyond measure.

The great secret, I think, is never to think of a dog as merely a pet, or a useful worker, or as part of the family, but as a character in his own right, inheriting all the innate instincts and working qualities for which the breed was originally evolved, and which have gradually become fixed throughout the generations. Unless he is educated by training and experience and allowed to develop those inherent qualities to the full, he will never become the dog he could be— but instead, in extreme instances, a crazy-mixed-up bundle of canine neurosis, or, in more normal cases, just another DOG.

Because of their age-long association with man, dogs tend to adapt themselves to their owners' wishes, but if these wishes are in constant conflict with the dog's extremely strong inherited instincts, he is willy-nilly almost bound to be schizophrenic as a direct result.

So that it is extremely silly, if it is nothing worse, to expect a working terrier to become a lap-dog (especially when there are so many breeds of toy dog to choose from instead), or a gun-dog to become a guard-dog, or a hound, bred for hunting hares, gazelles, foxes, boars, wolves or deer, to become a companion on suburban strolls round the crescents.

There are now so many different breeds available, and at prices to suit all incomes, that it is easily possible to find the right breed for your tastes and circumstances.

Chapter 15

SELLING A PUP

If you have established a good reputation as a reliable breeder, supplying strong, hardy, healthy, plucky puppies at a reasonable price, you should have absolutely no difficulty in selling as many as you want to. In fact, you will probably have a waiting list for your next litter. But until that reputation is made, probably your best method is to advertise them in the sporting, dog or local press, and for a slightly lower price than you can reasonably ask later.

Reasonable prices vary, but around £45 is about right. Emphasise that your litter is bred from working parents, of healthy stock, and are sound and typey. And don't forget your name, address and telephone number. It might be as well to add 'inspection invited, but by appointment, please', as prospective purchasers, in my experience, have an awkward habit of just turning up, from miles away, at very awkward times, and buying or selling a puppy is not a thing that should be undertaken in a hurry, lightly, wantonly or unadvisedly. The average life of a Jack Russell is about fourteen years, and that is a long time to have to live with a dog you have bought in a hurry on the spur of the moment.

Personally, I like people to write to me first, giving me some details about themselves and the home that my precious puppy will be going to. I also like to have time, after they arrive, to decide whether they are likely to be worthy owners or not.

Also, in the case of a Jack Russell, find out whether it will lead a normal country life, under normal working conditions, with people who know and understand the breed, or who have kept other working terriers, or whether it is condemned to spend the life of a lap-dog in a town flat six storeys up. In this last case, I most definitely will not sell it.

With a little practice, one can become amazingly skilful and tactful at refusing to sell a puppy, and I have several well-tried and proved methods, but if the worst comes to the worst, and nothing will dissuade them, try this one: Put either 'prices reasonable' or the magic words 'from £35' in your advertisement. You can then look them straight in the eye and allege that all the puppies you have left are well over £75 apiece. If they are still willing to pay that, they either deserve to have their puppy, or you can then take refuge in the last painful resort—just a plain refusal on the grounds that you do not consider they are suitable Jack Russell owners—and tell them why.

Jack Russells are not mere pets or lap-dogs. They are working terriers, and although they are, admittedly, extremely adaptable, cheerful and obliging, they will never realise their full potential in a town, nor will they ever be as happy in a town as they would be in the country. Another telling point is that a bored and frustrated dog becomes a mischievous dog—liable to go off on his own and find his own amusements—and these may not be in accordance with the local by-laws. If his prospective new owners want a pet or a lap-dog, or if elderly and disinclined for exercise, there are plenty of other breeds to choose from.

Unfortunately, the majority of those breeds, although eminently suitable in other ways, have one great draw-back—they are pretty expensive, compared with the Jack Russell. Nevertheless, tell them it is possible to buy a 'pet' puppy of almost any breed for a more realistic price from one of the big kennels that goes in mainly for show dogs. Quite often there is very little wrong with it, except that it is just too big, or too small, or too long in the back, or mismarked in some minor way that spoils its chances of ever becoming a Champion, and its breeder is only too glad to find it a good home.

And remember that a bad home for a Jack Russell might prove an ideal home for a Pug, or a Chihuahua or a Poodle.

I have found that quite frequently people turn up, wanting a puppy of a certain breed, without any clear idea of what becoming the owner of a dog of that breed involves. And quite often, once this is clearly explained to them, they become quite keen, and are perfectly willing to change their ways to conform to my idea of what the Ideal Owner should be. In several cases I have regular enthusiastic letters telling me how much they are enjoying their new way of life, and asking me to find a mate for their now adult dog as they want to begin breeding.

There is a lot more to selling a puppy than simply letting buyers choose one and write out a cheque!

I am never keen on allowing anyone to have a young puppy on approval—although I am with an older, trained dog. Puppies can be upset by the change, or by stupid handling or feeding, and, anyway, I do not think that it is possible to tell much about an eight-weeks-old puppy— beyond what you can see at your first visit, and after about twenty minutes' acquaintance. It takes time to settle down and develop. I will always, however, take a puppy back later if it really proves unsuitable, as I find that nine times out of ten it has just been badly handled, and very quickly turns into a reasonable dog when back at its old home and to the old routine.

When I first started as breeder, I used to get my vet to call when the puppies were ready to go, examine them, inoculate them against distemper and leptospirosis, and give each a certificate of soundness for its new owner, as well as a certificate of inoculation. I also, through my insurance agency, insured them all for one month after sale, for a small sum. I also always give a detailed diet sheet away with each puppy, and a few typewritten hints on training, or a similar pamphlet.

I also encourage new owners to get in touch with me as well as their vet if anything goes wrong. In other words, I endeavour to give after-sales-service—and this pays dividends in all sorts of ways from new friends to new converts to the breed.

All puppies, of course, should be wormed twice before they leave home and be healthy and sound.

There is nothing worse for a breeder's reputation than a dissatisfied customer, who can do far more harm than ten delighted ones can do good. As no dog is perfect, it is better to be quite honest about any failings, too, either in the puppies or their parents.

In the case of Jack Russells, especially with novice owners, hints on training, or the loan of a good book on this subject, is a sound policy, otherwise they may ruin a good puppy by entering it for foxes far too young, or even expecting it to deal with large and fierce rats at a far too tender age. Quite often, the new owners need just as much initial training as the puppy!

Warn them that a young puppy needs rest and sleep just as much as it needs food, and its own special box to retire to when it wants. Warn them, too, as some people, although well-intentioned, are pretty stupid at first, that a very young puppy has no control over its bowels and bladder, and give them a few hints about how to counteract this.

If you keep pedigrees, have one ready for them—and don't vaguely promise to send it on soon. It is also a good plan to give them a written guarantee of the working qualities of the parents, endorsed, if possible, by your local MFH—if your terriers have worked with his hunt, or by some disinterested person. It all helps.

Chapter 16

FOXES, RATS AND FERRETS

The original Jack Russells were bred and trained by their famous founder for one purpose only—fox-hunting.

Except for a comparatively brief period of seven years out of his long and active life, while he was the curate of George Nympton, in North Devon, from 1819 until 1826, when he took up otter-hunting for want of something better to do, fox-hunting, and fox-hunting alone, was his main recreation, love and joy.

His terriers were trained to run with the hounds on foot, to 'ware riot, and to do their stuff under any conditions. They were bred for brains, courage, stamina, hardihood and endurance, and they must have needed the Lot, as Jack Russell hunted his hounds from Barnstaple to Bodmin Moor, and in those days hound-vans, horse-boxes, and cars were unknown and unimagined.

His methods were all his own, and extremely successful, and seem to have consisted mainly in letting his young entry run with his older and more experienced terriers and learn from them. This, I still think, is the best way, but in these days it is not always practicable.

Since Jack Russell's day, his terriers have gradually become all-purpose working terriers, but their original virtues still remain. And I most sincerely hope that their present amazing popularity will not spoil them.

Jack Russells demonstrate their enthusiasm and readiness for a day's sport. It's head-first down the hole (*top left*), then a scramble and scrum to get the rats as they emerge—and not without argument as to which dog gets the prize.

Frankly, I don't think it will, as they are hard-headed little dogs of immense character, and it should take more than a popular craze to go to their heads. But, let me emphasise with every accent of literary persuasion I have at my command, they do need careful training to bring out the best in them.

Their very virtues are two-edged and can become vices in the wrong hands. The great secret of making a good Jack Russell is (a) never give any conflicting or stupid orders—in other words, *think* before you speak, (b) always remain cool, quiet and firm, and (c) ensure that your orders are carried out. Never let a Jack Russell get the better of you.

In spite of expert advice to the contrary, although I did occasionally resort to corporal punishment in my early days, it is now years since I hit or thrashed a dog. I now know that they work far better for love and respect than for any threats, fear or bribes. But they are no fools, and to control them properly you have got to understand your end of the job in hand beyond any shadow of canine doubt. You just cannot bluff 'em as I have proved time and time again.

The most convincing proof of this I ever remember was many years ago, when I went to help dig out some badgers that had become too much of a local nuisance to tolerate any longer. There were three of us in the digging party—myself, the local know-all, and a very quiet, shy, retiring chap of vast experience—each with terriers. Like all badger strongholds the sett was vast with infinite internal galleries and several exits. All the terriers were trained and experienced. Our object was not to kill the badgers, for whom two of us had a vast respect and liking, but to bag them and 'move them on' to another district, at least twenty miles away. (Even this treatment of badgers is quite illegal now.) The Brock is a gentle, unassuming creature if not provoked into aggression, when he can give a really terrifying account of himself, and one of the oldest inhabitants of the British Isles, and we wished him no ill.

The know-all was noisy, over-eager in siccing on his terriers and irritating. The quiet chap hardly opened his mouth. Yet it was significant that before the end of the dig every terrier present was taking its orders and advice from the quiet chap and ignoring the other. They just knew. I also learnt, during that dig, that when there is a job on hand terriers will forget about loyalty, and instinct will reign supreme. In other words, they will look to the man who knows and who can direct them aright, before their own master.

A terrier should be brought on by progressive stages and never asked to tackle anything beyond his capacity until he is fully mature. Eighteen months old is quite soon enough for foxes.

Sir Walter Scott, my compatriot and neighbour, in space if not in time, has summed up the whole art of training working terriers in the words of Dandy Dinmont:

'A bonny terrier that, sir, and a fell chiel at the vermin, I warrant him—that is, if he's been weel entered, for it a' lies in that.'

(And how right he was!)

'Really, sir,' said Brown, 'his education has been somewhat neglected, and his chief property is in being a pleasant companion.'

(And how wrong HE was! But how representative of many Jack Russell owners to this day.)

'Ay, sir! That's a pity, begging your pardon—it's a great pity, that—beast or body, education should aye be

minded. I have six terriers at home, forbye twa couple o'
slow hounds, five grews, an' a wheen ither dugs. There's
Auld Pepper, and Auld Mustard, and Young Pepper and
Young Mustard, and Little Pepper and Little Mustard. I
had them all regularly entered: first wi' the tods or
brocks—and now they fear nothing that ever cam' with a
hairy skin on't.'

Again, in my opinion, how right he was! A good working
dog can be ruined for life by being entered too soon to foxes,
who can be really savage when cornered.

He must be given time to mature and develop, and to gain
the necessary experience on lesser fry, such as rottens (rats),
and then graduate via stoats and weasels, until he is old
enough and ready to tackle his true end—foxes.

Unfortunately, the march of progress has almost elimi-
nated one of the most fruitful sources of giving a young dog
experience—the threshing mill. Should you be lucky enough
to find some fruitful source of rats—clearing of old timber
or straw stacks—try, if you can, to dissuade eager beavers
from assisting with shouts and sticks, and to leave the
dispatching to the terriers. And, incidentally, *never* take a
terrier ratting unless it has been previously inoculated against
leptospiral jaundice, as rat-bites can be lethal—and most rats
do bite.

Jack Russells, in common with most working terriers, are
madly excitable. They do not need any encouragement—
especially from outsiders—to do their stuff, but they do need
reassurance and calm, quiet support. If there is an army of
farm-workers and hangers-on as well as other dogs, they will
become confused, and not give of their best (to put it mildly)
so insist that your terrier (or terriers) are given a fair chance.
If you have only one untried youngster, an older, experienced
dog is a wonderful ally, but most Jack Russells take to rat-
killing like ducks to water and give an excellent account of

Above Not the most obvious of gun-dogs, Jack Russells are, nevertheless, extremely versatile.

Below Out with the guns and demonstrating retrieving skills.

themselves. After that, word goes round the grapevine like wildfire, and you will find yourself overwhelmed by invitations, via the local pub, to come along at the next opportunity. Rats are one of the farmer's worst enemies.

The age for ratting varies, both in dogs and expert opinion, but from nine months upwards is about the right age.

Don't worry if your Jack Russell is a slow starter. In my experience this is a good sign, as I have found that the more intelligent types do not rush in bald-headed, but tend to hang back and watch and learn before pitching in.

I am fully aware, and reckon that it is my bounden duty in a book of this type, to remind you that a lot of the experts recommend catching rats alive and letting your puppies kill them—but, quite frankly, my gorge rises at the idea. I cannot help having a soft spot for the hunted—even if it happens to be a rat, and if there is any killing to be done, I'd rather it was in a more sporting fashion. I know that Nature is red in tooth and claw, but wire traps are not natural anyway. I also know that rats are menaces, and must be eradicated at any cost, but I used to keep pet rats when I was young and really loved them. I also have a curious theory that you don't teach a sporting terrier to be sporting by unsporting methods.

Another excellent way of introducing your Jack Russell to his hereditary prey is during harvest time, when the combine harvesters have only about twenty square yards of corn island to cut. This is always full of a variety of game—from tiny shrew-mice to large hares—who stay there until the last moment and then bolt for safety and freedom. On these occasions you don't even have to ask—you can just turn up with the rest and wait for the psychological moment.

Entering to fox is trickier, unless you know the Master or the Huntsman, but the best way is to get up early in September on a cubbing morning, hang around with your terrier on a lead and await your chance. If you can, it is a good idea to get to know and memorise the different hunting horn calls, and to recognise the 'Gone to ground and need a terrier' one, which goes roughly: 'ta-ta, ta-ta-ta-ta, ta-ta, ta-ta-ta-ta, ta-ta-ta-ta,' which is probably just so much double-Dutch and means as much to the average reader as Bloch or Bruckner do to a pop fan.

The great thing about entering a terrier to an earth is to do it quietly, with the absolute minimum of noise and fuss. Jack Russells, after all, are bred for just this job and have generations of experienced ancestors behind them so that they do not have to be shown how. If you get excited yourself and start siccing him on, all he will do, in his effort to play up and oblige, is begin barking at nothing, which won't help him or anyone. Leave him alone and listen and he will let you know all right where he is and what he is doing once he reaches his cub.

As terriers seldom emerge unscathed, and as fox bites can be nasty, it is advisable to carry a first-aid kit with you on these occasions and cope with any wounds immediately the terrier emerges.

A fox generally snaps, so that you can expect a number of small puncture wounds on the face and head, which should be dressed with iodine, TCP, diluted Dettol or some such antiseptic.

Before beginning to work with ferrets, it is a good idea to let the terrier get accustomed to their sight and smell, and to teach him that they are privileged persons that must not be worried or killed. Our old gamekeeper used to be a great believer in letting a young terrier get bitten by a ferret, in order to teach him to leave them alone—but I never agreed, as I reckon it is far more likely to make him want to retaliate and attack and kill the ferret.

Whilst the ferrets are working—either in rat or rabbit holes, the terriers must be taught to stay quietly waiting for their quarry to bolt. A slip lead is a good thing—provided that you have practised beforehand how to slip it swiftly, as the rat or rabbit can bolt out of the hole like greased lightning, and, as the terrier generally lunges forward at the psychological moment, the handler has to be an adept at his job. Of course, nets at the mouths of the holes are better, if less sporting, but working with ferrets is a wonderful way of training young dogs and much more sporting than nets.

When ferreting, I have always squatted down and held my terriers between my legs, with my hands clasped in front of them. By this method you are in close communion with your dog and can keep him silent by whispering almost noiselessly to him. Murmurs like: 'Steady—wait for it—ssh! Quietly now—steady,' and so on. Then, when the rat or rabbit bolts, all you do is let him go. No fuss with leads or slip collars.

One last word of warning: if you take your terrier ratting, always wear slacks or breeches tucked either into your Wellingtons or into your socks so that the rats cannot run up your trouser legs or skirt. This happens far more often than one might inagine, and, although it may be excruciatingly funny to the rest of the party, it is no joke for you.

When I was young, I once persuaded a prim and elderly governess, who wore skirts almost down to her ankles, to join a rat-hunt. The inevitable happened and a rat ran up her leg, underneath the capacious, tent-like skirt. She very nearly died on the spot of heart failure.

Chapter 17

THE TREATMENT OF AILMENTS AND INJURIES

The Jack Russell is a tough, hardy, healthy little dog, and if he is properly fed, exercised and looked after, he will probably give you little worry or trouble, beyond dressing the occasional cut or wound, all his life.

However, as forewarned is forearmed, it is a good thing to be prepared for all emergencies by knowing about them before they crop up—as they can do even in the best homes.

The golden rule is when in doubt to send for your veterinary surgeon—and this also applies to any deep or large cut which may need stitching. Although I have occasionally stitched a cut myself in a real emergency only a vet or a doctor can do it properly.

See also Chapter 10 Whelping Complications and Chapter 11 Bringing up the Babies.

ADDER BITES

Jack Russells, because they attack snakes, may be bitten on the head or neck; or they may stand on a sleeping adder, and get bitten on a paw.

In any case they must be rushed to the nearest hospital or veterinary surgery as soon as possible, and kept as still and quiet as possible. There are various injections and serums that can help. The dose of anti-venene is not according to the size of the animal, but according to the amount of venom injected when it was bitten. It is a wise course to telephone first to find out if an antidote is available as, if not, another surgery may be suggested.

Vipers and adders have very long fangs, and inject their venom into the muscle, and the damaged capillaries and delay in clotting cause severe haemorrhage; fulminating infections and gangrene are also common, as the venom remains active for days. Death, if it occurs, is due to haemorrhages and pulmonary oedema (i.e. bleeding internally, and water on the lungs and respiratory system).

Although opening the wound further, with a knife, and sucking it (as long as the sucker has no ulcers or sore places on the mouth or tongue) may help in the case of some snakebites, it is not recommended in the case of *Viperriidae* (or adders); neither is a tourniquet advisable, except in the event of a bite from a very large adder.

Alcohol and exercise both help to make matters worse, by dispersing the venom further through the blood-stream.

If the head or neck are bitten, a tracheotomy may be necessary to prevent suffocation from the swelling, as the venom liberates histamines, which cause this.

Symptoms are swelling at the place of the bite, and the dog becoming particularly lethargic and drowsy.

BROKEN BONES
Of course, these are again the vet's business, but it is possible to straighten a broken leg, and fix a temporary splint which may prevent a simple fracture from becoming a complicated one until the vet arrives, or you can take the dog to his surgery. Broken legs, especially in young dogs, heal quickly, and do not affect future activity to any great degree.

CANINE DISTEMPER
This is one of the four major infectious diseases to affect dogs. The others are canine hepatitis, leptospirosis and

parvovirus. It is a particularly nasty disease with two distinct phases, acute and chronic.

In the acute phase the dog exhibits all the clinical signs of nasal discharge, dry harsh cough, diarrhoea, vomiting and loss of appetite. This in turn leads to fits. In the chronic phase, hard-pad and nervous signs are the main findings. The outlook for distemper cases is extremely poor but fluid therapy and symptomatic treatments may effect a cure in a very small proportion of cases. A dog with these symptoms must be taken to a veterinary surgeon at once.

Inoculation with distemper vaccine is highly effective, and is a must for all puppies.

CANKER

A tiny mite that infects the inside of the ears. It can easily be detected by the dog's behaviour, as it shakes its ears and scratches; also one can hear a liquid sound when it shakes, and there is a peculiar smell. The treatment is to apply ear-drops, obtained from the veterinary surgeon for the purpose. Or, in less severe cases, a powder can be puffed down the ear-hole.

CONSTIPATION

Constipation can mean anything from a stoppage, caused by swallowing a foreign body or object, to merely a lazy bowel motion. An unsuitable diet with inadequate roughage can cause constipation and so can lack of exercise. Very often the dog, if given free access to grass and herbs, will cure itself. Cod-liver oil, given regularly in small doses, is a good preventive, as is water to drink. So is olive oil. Liquid paraffin is all right occasionally but as it absorbs Vitamin D it should not be given too often or for a long period. Castor oil, although useful for evacuating a definite block, has a back-kick which actually causes constipation, as it is an astringent. Normally a constipated dog will come right, if the condition

A prospect of sport and some nasty bites—ratting with ferrets
under a chicken run.

does not last for longer than twenty-four hours, but if it is
accompanied by vomiting, shivering, pain, and the passage
of blood, then get the vet immediately.

CUTS AND WOUNDS
These should never be neglected, and quite a lot of handlers
of working terriers carry a small bottle of diluted antiseptic
with which to treat them on the spot. Terriers frequently get
cut on barbed wire, bits of tin, sticking-out nails, and sharp
edges when they are too excited about the immediate job on
hand to be careful. Generally, they lick cuts themselves and
so heal them, but a watchful eye is necessary, and a working
terrier should always be carefully examined at the end of the
day for any bites, scratches, or wounds, and carefully disinfected and dressed, more particularly if they are in a spot
where the dog cannot reach to lick, such as a torn ear, the
neck, or on the face and jaw.

All burrs and thistles should be removed from a rough coat and the mud brushed out so that the dog can settle down comfortably for the night.

DIARRHOEA

Diarrhoea is a very common ailment and should always be taken seriously. In the majority of cases it will probably clear up quite easily but it may be a symptom of a more serious problem. Withholding food for 24 hours may effect a cure, but failing this get veterinary attention. Diarrhoea is often accompanied by vomiting and sometimes, as a result of this, dehydration occurs. This is life threatening and will need treatment with fluid therapy by a veterinary surgeon. Nursing is of great importance in cases of prolonged diarrhoea.

DISTEMPER

See Canine Distemper

FITS

Fits can be due to several causes and can vary from a mild twitching and spasm to foaming at the mouth and insensibility. In lactating bitches, fits are nearly always due to eclampsia, and an immediate injection of calcium borogluconate may be essential to save her life. Eclampsia is a calcium deficiency, due to heavy lactation, and generally occurs (if it occurs at all) during the third week after the puppies are born—especially if there is a large litter, or the bitch has had several pregnancies, or two pregnancies too close together.

Fits in puppies can be caused by worms, or teething, or even over-excitement, or a bad fright, but they are a danger signal nevertheless and should never occur in healthy puppies of healthy parentage. They can also be caused by incipient kidney disease, acute infections and toxic conditions, and if any of your dogs ever has a fit—*send for the vet*. Meanwhile keep it isolated, quiet, reassured by your presence, and in semi-darkness. An aspirin can help—but remember to tell the vet, when he arrives, if you have given any sedative, as it may mask some of the symptoms he is looking for.

FLEAS AND LICE

Fleas are very common and becoming more so. They must never be underestimated. The flea is not host specific like the louse. The real problem with fleas is that they do not live on the host which, of course, presents problems in treatment. With lice a bath with an insecticidal shampoo will usually cure the problem, but fleas lay their eggs in cracks in floorboards and carpets. Consequently re-infestation is very likely. The clinical signs are itching, scurfy coat with broken hairs and if the dog is allergic, a wet dermatitis may develop. Treatment of this is best carried out by a veterinary surgeon.

Once fleas are in a kennel they are very difficult to eradicate. Treatment may have to include fumigation of the premises and destruction of all bedding materials, although nowadays sprays are available for use on furniture and bedding etc. It is also worth remembering that the flea is the intermediate host of the dog tapeworm, which makes them potentially more than just a nuisance.

HARD-PAD
See Canine Distemper

HARVEST MITES

Although almost invisible tiny red creatures, they can also cause trouble during the months of July, August and September. They are actually larvae which are found in growing corn and tall grass, and can cause intense irritation by getting into the folds of the skin, or burrowing into it, and this in its turn causes scratching, sores and secondary infections. The best way to deal with them is to scratch the top off the place and apply powdered sulphur.

INOCULATION
The standard inoculation, which must be given to all puppies, covers the four principal dog diseases: infectious canine hepatitis, leptospirosis, canine distemper (hard-pad) and parvovirus disease. Recently there has been much discussion in veterinary circles about the best time for puppies to be given the inoculations, so ask your vet who will be able to advise you.

The first three diseases seem to cause little problem when the puppy is inoculated at three months. Parvovirus does, however, pose problems due to the persistence of passive protection from the pup's mother. A puppy derives passive protection from its mother's immune system via the placenta and her milk, and although it seems that there is no protection against hepatitis, leptospirosis and distemper after 11 weeks, protection against parvovirus may last as long as 16 weeks. So, once again, ask your vet. An annual booster injection is also essential. And if your dog(s) have to go to kennels, all the good ones require up-to-date certificates of vaccination.

KENNEL COUGH
A highly contagious though not serious condition. If your dog has a persistent cough that has no obvious cause, such as something stuck in its throat, it could be kennel cough. Ring your vet for advice first, because taking an infectious dog to a crowded surgery could mean that all the other dogs there get the disease.

LENS LUXATION
This is an eye conditon to which terriers seem particularly prone, although the condition is not common. The dog will

rub or paw at its eye, and the white part will show quite a lot of redness. The affected eye also looks larger than the other and has a rather vacant look about it. If your dog shows these symptoms take it to the vet as soon as possible.

LEPTOSPIROSIS
See Inoculation

LICE
See Fleas and Lice

MANGE
There are three types of mange: scabies, demodectic mange and cheylitiella.

Scabies, which is caused by *Sarcoptes* or *Psoroptes* mites, is not as common as it used to be. It is highly contagious and causes crusty lesions over the whole body, but more commonly on the feet and edges of the ears. Demodectic mange is caused by a parasite (*Demodex canis*) which is found in the hair follicles of most dogs. In some dogs it seems that it becomes pathogenic, causing severe scaly dermatitis on the face and legs. Lesions, however, can be found anywhere on the body. Occasionally a pustular form of the disease occurs, with small abscesses forming in association with the infected hair follicles.

Cheylitiella (*Cheylitiella parasitavorax*) causes a mild skin condition characterised by excessive scurf or dandruff on the coat. All these conditions are potentially very debilitating and if you suspect one of them consult a vet immediately.

PARVOVIRUS DISEASE
This is another of the four main diseases of dogs. It is characterised by vomiting, bloody diarrhoea, dehydration and rapid weight loss in puppies. It is highly contagious in puppies which have not been inoculated. Treatment is by

fluid therapy and antibiotics, though the mortality rate is high. Vaccination is effective if done within the manufacturers' guidelines.

RABIES (HYDROPHOBIA)

Rabies is an acute, horrible, and almost invariably fatal disease, affecting animals, birds and man. It is caused by a neurotropic virus, accompanied by nervous symptoms. The virus is excreted mainly through the saliva; generally by a bite, but sometimes through licking. Although the infection cannot penetrate an intact skin, it can pass through an intact membrane.

Even before the appearance of clinical symptoms, the virus is present, in the saliva.

'Classical' rabies, in dogs, has three stages:

1. The prodomal stage, with alterations in behaviour: the animal is moody, restless, frightened, irritable, and tends to hide. There may also be signs of depraved appetite.
2. The second, excited, stage occurs after 1–3 days. The animal is excited, aggressive, and has an urge to escape and roam about. It attacks, bites, and has involuntary movements. Depression and paralytic symptoms lead to stage 3.
3. The paralytic stage: general dullness sets in; there is paralysis of the lower jaw, the oesophagus, and the rest of the body. Death mercifully follows, about the 5th–8th day.

There are, unfortunately, other forms of rabies, which are not so easy to diagnose, and some atypical forms are prevalent in Germany, especially the so-called 'dumb rabies', which are characterised by absence of the usual excitement and aggressiveness; the animal is weak, has no appetite, vomits, and has diarrhoea in the early stages, until the onset of paralysis and coma and death. The atypical period can last for a week, or longer, during which time the saliva is infectious.

There is no cure for rabies. Human beings who have been bitten by rabid animals, or who have come in contact with infected material, can be protected by vaccination (a long, highly painful and unpleasant procedure) but, so far, post-infective vaccination has proved useless for dogs.

Preventive vaccination for dogs is, as yet, of doubtful efficiency.

Rabies is a notifiable disease. Stringent precautions are taken to ensure that no dog enters this country without undergoing a period of quarantine in approved kennels, and heavy fines or imprisonment are imposed on anyone who is caught trying to evade the law.

RINGWORM

Ringworm is caused by a fungus which is found in hair follicles. It causes a round scaly lesion which is not usually itchy. Fortunately, it is easy to treat with drugs which a vet will be happy to supply.

Ringworm is highly contagious to humans and other animals, although not a particularly serious condition in itself.

ROUNDWORM

The roundworm is pointed at both ends, and up to six inches long. All puppies should be wormed, by pills on a vet's prescription, within the first few weeks of their life, and again ten days later, to eradicate the eggs which by this time will have hatched and which will continue to infest the puppy if it is not dosed twice.

However, it is just possible that a puppy may have been missed. In which case the first symptoms are a variable appetite, a pot-bellied look, dry coat, running eyes and intermittent diarrhoea, often with mucus or worms present in the stools.

TAPEWORM

The tapeworm is a terror, as unless the head is detached and destroyed it will continue to flourish and grow new segments. Rabbits and fleas are the most common carriers, but as the segments of the worm are evacuated by the dog or the host, each carries an egg, which can be picked up and eaten by other dogs, who will then become the hosts of a tapeworm, in their turn, and the cycle can go on for ever unless firmly and effectively dealt with—again by a veterinary surgeon, please, and not by any amateur doctoring with 'remedies' bought over the counter, however strongly recommended. It is essential that the head (the smallest part of the worm) is detached, or it will grow again—sometimes to the length of several feet. This attaches itself to the wall of the intestine by a multitude of microscopic hooks, and grows yards of flat segments, which break off, and can look rather like squashed rice as they are evacuated through the anus. A healthy tapeworm means a far from healthy dog, but since a tapeworm requires an intermediate host one dog cannot directly infect another.

TICKS

Are more common, especially in the country, and must also be watched for and exterminated as they too suck the blood and can cause big trouble—especially anaemia. As they are large (about half an inch long) and grey, they can be fairly easily spotted in the smooth-haireds and whites, but are more difficult in the roughs, as they seem to choose the coloured spots, where they are less visible. They attach themselves to the dog with pincers, and a drop of turpentine will cause them to curl up and drop off. Or they can be removed by hand and burnt, care being taken to see the head of the tick is completely removed, or it will cause inflammation.

Incidentally—*all* parasites must be collected on a sheet of newspaper and burnt, or dropped into a bucket of water and paraffin and drowned, or they will crawl away and survive and eventually reattach themselves.

Chapter 18

PARSON JACK RUSSELL

The Rev. John Russell was born in Devonshire in 1795. Except for the time spent at Oxford taking his degree, he lived in Devonshire, worked in Devonshire, hunted in Devonshire, and finally died in Devonshire in 1883.

Right up until almost the very end of his long and active eighty-eight years he was a man of tireless energy and immense vitality, which he divided between his parishioners, his terriers, his hounds, his horses, his family, his parish, and his hunting.

It is puzzling that a man of his undoubted gifts of energy, oratory, zeal and learning never rose higher in his chosen profession than curate. The reason may have been lack of ambition, but more probably it was because of the unfortunate fact that his immediate ecclesiastical superior, the Bishop of Exeter, strongly disapproved of sporting parsons.

Because of Parson Jack's tremendous reputation as a sportsman, an MFH, and a breeder of hunt terriers, his work as a curate is inclined to be overlooked (as it apparently was by the Bishop of Exeter). Nevertheless the few records that remain show him to have been a good and conscientious minister, much loved by all his people, and one, moreover, who did wonders to improve his church and parish.

Although he must have worked well and hard at Blundell's School, Tiverton, Devon, and had a good enough brain to win an exhibition to Exeter College, Oxford, as well as a medal for elocution, yet he narrowly escaped being expelled when the headmaster discovered that he and a school-friend were keeping a small pack of four-and-a-half couple of foxhounds with a neighbouring blacksmith.

And though he took a good degree at Oxford, well within the required period (his exhibition only lasted for four years), the authorities there considered that he spent far too much time and money from his small allowance on fox-hunting. Nor did they approve of his prowess as a heavy-weight boxer.

It was while he was still at Oxford that he bought his first 'Jack Russell' Terrier—the now famous bitch, Trump—from the Marston milkman, thereby laying the corner-stone of his temple of fame.

He was ordained in 1819 and nominated to the curacy of the parish of George Nympton, near South Molton, in Devon, at a salary of sixty pounds a year. To quote his friend and biographer Davis: 'That Russell entered on the work of ministry with a due sense of the sacred office and his own responsibility will, no doubt, be questioned by many who have only heard of his fame in the hunting field. But if an ever-earnest readiness to visit the sick and world-weary; to adminster consolation to all who needed it; to relieve the wants of his poorer brethren however poor himself; to preach God's Word with fervour; to plead in many a neighbouring pulpit whenever invited to do so; if such things be of good report and carry any weight, no human being can say of him—though he would be the first to say it of himself—that his mission as a Christian minister had been altogether that of an unprofitable servant.'

It was during his time at George Nympton that he took up otter-hunting, with small success, until he bought a hound called Racer from a neighbouring farmer, who soon taught the rest.

Engraving of the full-length portrait of the Rev. John Russell in his favourite dress: top boots and hunting clothes.

In 1826 he married Miss Penelope Bury, the daughter of Admiral and Mrs Bury of Dennington House, near Barnstaple, a most admirable helpmate who shared all his love of country life and hunting, and who, when the egregious Bishop of Exeter demanded that Jack Russell gave up the Mastership of his pack, was quite willing to take them over in his stead.

They had two sons. The first, John Bury, was born on 29 May, 1827, but to his parents' great sorrow, only lived for a year and died on 31 May, 1828. The second, Richard Bury, was born on 23 August, 1828—just three months after his tiny brother had been buried in Iddesleigh churchyard. Richard Bury grew up to follow in his parents' footsteps as a sportsman, was Colonel of the North Devon Militia, a JP for North Devon, and died in the same year as his father in 1883.

About this time Jack Russell became curate to his father at Iddesleigh, where he managed to collect a small pack of foxhounds, 'hunting,' as he himself relates, 'anything I could find around my own garden', as the bounds of his maiden country were confined to a very limited area. He had also a hard struggle at first to persuade his parishioners not to kill every fox they found. However, in time, he had them all as keen as he was himself.

After six years at Iddesleigh the family moved to Tordown, in the parish of Swymbridge, on the opposite side of the valley to Mrs Russell's parents at Dennington House. The following year, 1833, Jack Russell was appointed the Perpetual Curate of Swymbridge and Landkey—at an annual income of £180 per annum, out of which he had to pay a curate for Landkey, meet perpetual calls upon his generosity from a large population of poor parishioners, and bring up his son. Nevertheless, he not only managed to do all this but to improve his parish and church out of all recognition during the forty-five years he was there. New schools were built and established, a new chapel was built at a distant hamlet, called Traveller's Rest, the parish church was restored at a cost of £3,000, and, to quote Russell's own words, 'there was only one service every Sunday morning and evening alternately with Landkey, whereas now, I am thankful to say, we have four services every Sunday in Swymbridge alone'.

His services, other than ecclesiastical or ministerial, were much in demand, as his fame grew, at agricultural and hound shows, as a judge, and it was at one of these, the Royal Agricultural Society of England, at Plymouth in 1865, that he was invited to dine with the Prince of Wales, later Edward VII. This was the beginning of a life-long friendship with the royal family, and when Russell died the Prince of Wales bought a painting of Trump, which now hangs in the harness room at Sandringham. It was while he was staying at Sandringham that he danced the old year out and the new year (1874) in with the Princess of Wales—later Queen Alexandra.

He also preached in Sandringham Church, having been commanded to 'put a sermon in his pocket before he left home'.

In the autumn of that same year, 1874, the greatest sorrow of his long life fell upon him with the illness and death of his beloved wife, who died on New Year's Day, 1875—almost a year before their Golden Wedding anniversary.

Russell was overwhelmed with grief, but busied himself with working and preaching for charitable causes. 'I am worked to death,' he wrote to a friend, 'at this season of the year [November]; going about from church to church on week days as well as Sundays, preaching and begging for the North Devon Infirmary and similar institutions, and finding, when I come home, heaps of letters to answer, but no one there to cheer me in my labour—alone! alone!'

In July, 1879, when he was eighty-four, he was offered the living of Black Torrington, about which he wrote to Mr

Davis, 'Tell me, my dear old friend, what *shall* I do about Black Torrington? I cannot live on £220 a year here, which is all I shall have after I have paid a certain annuity for another three or four years. Black Torrington is a clear £500 a year, and there is a good house; but then it is neither Tordown nor Exmoor, and by the time I have settled in there, I shall perhaps be called upon to leave it again for Swymbridge churchyard! What shall I do? How can I leave my own people, with whom I have lived in peace and happiness for half a century? It will be a bitter pill to swallow, if it must be taken; but it will be my poverty, and not my will that will consent to it.'

An old parishioner, John Squire of Accot, told him that if he left Swymbridge it would not be long before he was back again—in the churchyard. However it was three years before this prophecy was fulfilled. Three most active and busy years, too, although what Russell wryly described as his 'house-warming' was a sad affair; just after his new stables were completed they were burnt down and 'in an hour and half became a heap of ruins. There were two horses, Simon and a valuable Irish mare, in them, beside two terriers. Alas! they are all dead.'

Before he left Swymbridge, his friends, headed by the Prince of Wales, and his parishioners presented him with a testimonial of nearly £800, 'for his kindly work as a clergyman in his late parish, and for his charity and Christian love'.

His magnificently robust health began to fail at long last, and although he was still hunting in the autumn of 1882 his anxious friends observed him 'much broken and showing manifest tokens of failing strength'.

His faithful and devoted house-keeper, Mary Cocking, wrote to cancel an engagement for him in October, 'I am grieved to say my dear master is very unwell, and in bed since Sunday. Three doctors are attending him, and I fear they think him *very, very* ill.'

Although, thanks to his temperate habits and magnificent constitution, he rallied enough to revisit his beloved Exmoor, he never recovered, and on 28 April, 1883, in his eighty-eighth year, he slipped peacefully away to his long rest.

He was buried at Swymbridge, with over a thousand mourners, including his old parishioners, who, 'weeping as they went', filled his grave with the wild flowers that he loved.

INDEX